Dedication

To Bethany Joy—
my complement, companion, and coheir

CONTENTS

FOREWORD

The apostle Paul wrote, "[We] glory in tribulations, knowing that tribulation produces perseverance; and perseverance, character; and character, *hope*. Now hope does not disappoint."

Hope for the Christian is not just a vague wish for something that may or may not happen ("I hope it will rain"). Christian hope has little to do with earthly optimism. But the hope of which the New Testament speaks is a firm and solid expectation of that which will *surely* come to pass in eternity—including the promise of Christ's return (Titus 2:13); the promise that we will be like Him (1 John 3:2–3); the promise that we will be partakers in His glory (Colossians 1:27); and the promise that we shall dwell with Him forever, free from the curse of sin (Revelation 22:3–5). True hope stems from the unshakable confidence that God is absolutely faithful to His promises, and therefore all those promises are as sure and certain as God Himself.

So hope is a forward-looking, far-reaching, heavenly perspective. It is not dependent on earthly realities. Indeed, a preoccupation with worldly and material ambitions will actually erode Christian hope.

But hope is absolutely vital to our spiritual survival. John Bunyan wrote, "Hope has a thick skin and will endure many a blow; it will put on patience as a vestment, it will wade through a sea of blood, it will endure all things if it be of the right kind, for the joy that is set before it. Hence patience is called 'patience of hope,' because it is hope that makes the soul exercise patience and long-suffering under the cross, until the time comes to enjoy the crown."

Of the three supreme virtues—faith, hope, and love (1 Corinthians 13:13)—hope is the most neglected. The volumes that have been written about faith and love would fill a small library, but solid, in-depth biblical studies on hope are surprisingly rare. That's why I am thankful for this marvelous work by Nathan Busenitz. Comprehensively biblical, sound and thorough, yet warm and practical, this is a wonderful resource for pastors and laypeople alike—a reminder of the importance of hope to every Christian and a refreshing study of the many benefits and blessings that we enjoy because of the hope that is set before us.

Although hope is cultivated by hardship and trial, it is the sweetest of Christian virtues. In fact, hope is the very thing that enables us to endure every trial with our joy intact.

Thus Peter speaks of "a *living* hope" (1 Peter 1:3). And the writer of Hebrews says, "This hope we have as an anchor of the soul, both sure and steadfast" (Hebrews 6:19 NKJV). Hope is a *firm* anchor for every believer's soul. In fact, Scripture describes Christians as those "who have fled for refuge to lay hold of the hope set before us" (Hebrews 6:18 NKJV). Christ *is* our hope (1 Timothy 1:1)—He is both the object and the source of our hope. Scripture also refers to God as "the God of hope" (Romans 15:13).

So authentic Christianity is all about hope. The whole of the Christian life is infused with hope, empowered by hope, and buoyed up by hope—no matter how fiercely the tempests of this life may assault us. That is why the character and the outlook of every Christian always ought to exude hope. This is a powerful testimony to a hopeless world.

As you read this book, may your heart and mind be filled with fresh hope, and "may the God of hope fill you with all joy and peace in believing, that you may abound in hope by the power of the Holy Spirit" (Romans 15:13 NKJV).

JOHN MACARTHUR

SETTING THE
STAGE

The Basis and Essence of Hope

CHAPTER 1

A HOPE THAT WILL NOT DISAPPOINT

Finding True Hope in a Hopeless World

No king is saved by the size of his army; no warrior escapes by his great strength.

A horse is a vain hope for deliverance; despite all its great strength it cannot save.

But the eyes of the LORD are on those who fear him,

on those whose hope is in his unfailing love,

to deliver them from death and keep them alive in famine.

PSALM 33:16–19

Everyone hopes in something. For some it is a healthy financial portfolio. For others it is a stable and enjoyable career. Still more find their hope in relationships and family. Yet the Bible offers an infinitely more secure Source of hope. . .God Himself.

As Christians, we can often get caught up in the false hopes of this world. Many times, it is not until we face hardship, adversity, and maybe even death that we remember to look to God's promises for a proper perspective on life. Yet, by focusing on the divine guarantees of His Word, we can find great comfort and joy even in the most difficult circumstances. After all, true hope is comprised of God's promises to us. Consider the following illustration:

Charles E. Fuller, a well-known radio evangelist of the mid-twentieth century, announced one day that his sermon the following Sunday would be on "Heaven." As he prepared his radio message that week, Fuller received a letter from an elderly man who knew that he was soon to die. Here is part of that letter:

> Next Sunday you are to talk about "Heaven." I am interested in that land because I have held a clear title to a bit of property there for over 55 years. I did not buy it. It was given to me without money and without price. But the donor purchased it for me at a tremendous sacrifice. I am not holding it for speculation, since the title is not transferable. It is not a vacant lot. . . . Termites can never undermine its foundations for they rest upon the Rock of Ages. Fire cannot destroy it. Floods cannot wash it away. No locks or bolts will ever be placed upon its doors, for no vicious person can ever enter that land where my dwelling stands, now almost completed and ready for me to enter and abide in peace eternally without fear of being ejected. There is a valley of deep shadow between the place where I live in California and that to which I shall journey in a very short time. I cannot reach my home in the City of God without passing through the dark valley of shadows. But I am not afraid, because the best friend that I ever had went through the same valley alone long, long ago and drove away all the gloom. He has stuck by me through thick and thin since we first became acquainted 55 years ago, and I hold His promise in printed form, never to forsake, nor to leave me alone. He will be with me as I walk through the valley of the shadows, and I shall not lose my way when He is with me. I hope to hear your sermon on Heaven next Sunday from my home,

but I have no assurance that I shall be able to do so. My ticket to heaven has no date marked for the journey—no return coupon—and no permit for baggage. Yes, I am ready to go and may not be here while you are talking next Sunday, but I shall meet you there someday.[1]

As I read that letter, I pictured that man—bent and shaking, his body wasted, his face wrinkled, his brow furrowed. From an earthly perspective, he is little more than skin on skeleton, a hopeless invalid. Yet, something in his eyes speaks of a hope of which this world knows nothing. There, between the thick eyebrows and the weathered cheeks sparkles a confidence that he, a soon passing mortal, will embrace life everlasting on the other side of the grave. In fact, I can't help imagining how that man is doing today, this very moment, in heaven. With the cares and sorrows of this life past, he enjoys a state of perpetual perfection, delighting daily in the presence of Christ.

The image I see when I think of that man is sharply contrasted with another account I recently found. Although several years old, its implications gripped me as I read it.

As Vice President George Bush represented the U.S. at the funeral of former Soviet leader Leonid Brezhnev, Bush was deeply moved by a silent protest carried out by Brezhnev's widow. She stood motionless by the coffin until seconds before it was closed. Then, just as the soldiers touched the lid, Brezhnev's wife performed an act of great courage and hope, a gesture that must surely rank as one of the most profound acts of civil disobedience ever committed: She reached down and made the sign of the cross on her husband's chest.

There in the citadel of secular, atheistic power, the

wife of the man who had run it all hoped that her hus-
band was wrong. She hoped that there was another life,
and that that life was best represented by Jesus, who
died on the cross, and that the same Jesus might yet have
mercy on her husband.[2]

A man without hope leaving behind a widow who hopes that her
husband is wrong. What a tragic picture this is of how many in the
world live each day.

A HOPELESS WORLD

Each year approximately 23 million Americans claim to suffer from
anxiety disorders, 17.5 million struggle with clinical depression,
530,000 actually attempt suicide, and countless others endure daily
feelings of fear and hopelessness. Airline passengers worry about the
safety of their flights; mourners grieve despondently at the loss of
loved ones; patients agonize over the dangers of surgery or the dead-
liness of their conditions; businesspeople fret because of their many
corporate decisions; and collegians cower at the uncertain future of
their careers. No wonder stress, worry, depression, and guilt run
rampant in our culture. The clock is ticking, life is short, and people
are looking for a safe place in which to put their trust.

Unfortunately, feelings of uncertainty and anguish are not the
sole property of secular culture. In fact, 62 percent of evangelical
Christians in America are concerned about the future, and 20 percent are "searching for meaning and purpose in life."[3] Amidst sickness, suffering, and doubt, many in today's church are following the
worldly minded down a hopeless path. The promises of God, as
given in His Word, are either no longer enough or no longer understood by those who claim the name of Christ. As a result, believers

look for other avenues in which to hope—money, relationships, possessions, amusement, power, or position. Each is worshiped as a potential source of security. Each promises a level of satisfaction and rest, yet each ultimately disappoints.

So, the question naturally arises. If there is nothing on this earth that can offer true hope, does true hope even exist? After all, many in this world are quick to tell us that there are no absolutes, so there can be no absolute hope. Hope is relative, like everything else. Even the word "hope" today carries no sense of certainty. Comments such as "I hope I win the lottery" or "I hope it doesn't rain tomorrow" flood contemporary conversations, evidencing both the whimsical and unfounded desires of many today. In modern society, hope is a dream or a chance, a penny tossed carelessly into a fountain. It guarantees nothing and instills no confidence. It is a shooting star, a rabbit's foot, or a broken wishbone. . .it is a "hope," but nothing more.

The Biblical Definition of Hope

In contrast to the worldly version of hope, the Bible says that there really is such a thing as true hope—a hope that is sure. In fact, Hebrews 11:1, a verse primarily defining faith, says, "Now faith is being sure of what we hope for and certain of what we do not see." And Romans 8:24 adds that "hope that is seen is no hope at all." Putting these two verses together, we see that hope refers to the promises of God (of which we can be sure) even when the fulfillment of those promises is still in the future—or unseen. Consequently, faith clings to the divine assurances of Scripture, refusing to let go of them even in the midst of dire circumstances. In other words, *when we hope in God, we fix our eyes on His promises rather than on personal circumstances.* And, because these guarantees come from God Himself (Titus 1:2), believers can be confident that their hope will never be disappointed (Romans 5:5). The hope of resurrection, the hope of heaven, and the hope of being like Christ are not examples of wishful thinking—they are divine guarantees. They are realities, not whimsical desires; they are absolutes, not possibilities; they are true, and they have bearing on our lives.

The problem is, unfortunately, that many Christians suffer from spiritual nearsightedness. All they can see is the world immediately around them. They see fancy cars, new furniture, big offices, scholarly achievement, and hefty bank accounts. . .and they want the same things for themselves. Not surprisingly, they spend their time pursuing the pleasures of this world, simply forgetting about the fact that eternity is a lot longer than seventy or eighty years. God's Word, however, serves as spiritual spectacles—getting our lives back in line with reality. When we set our minds on the truths of Scripture, our focus automatically shifts from the short time we have on this planet to our eternal destiny; our perspective is completely changed. After all, even God's promises for this life—such as the hope of continued spiritual growth and the hope of His provision and protection—foreshadow the promises that await us in the life to come. So, until we put on our biblical eyeglasses and embrace God's eternal promises, we will never be able to truly anchor ourselves in the present.

For example, imagine for a moment that you were suddenly diagnosed with an incurable disease. From an earthly standpoint, your situation is desperate. There is nothing you can do—despite the money in your bank account, the love of your family, the promotion at your job, or the nice house you own. In the world's eyes, hopelessness is all you have because, from a temporal perspective, death is inescapable.

Yet, imagine the same situation from a heavenly point of view. As a believer, you know that physical death is only the beginning. God has promised that to be absent from the body is to be present with Christ (2 Corinthians 5:8); that those who die in Christ will be raised together with Him (1 Thessalonians 4:16); that heavenly reward awaits those who have been faithful (Ephesians 6:8); that all believers will be conformed into the likeness of Christ (1 Corinthians 15:49); that physical death will complete the process of sanctification (Galatians 5:5); and so on. Death is no longer seen as hopeless, but rather as the much awaited transition from the temporal to the eternal. It is, for the believer, the doorway to Paradise—a doorway which can be embraced because of the God-given promises that undergird our hope.

Founded in Hope

Even before death comes knocking, true hope—properly understood—affects every single area of life. It is a totally new perspective—one that holds on to the eternal promises of God Himself in order to manage the temporal concerns of life on earth. Hope takes God at His Word, letting His guarantees guide every decision and action; hope may not change your circumstances, but it will change the way you view them.

As believers, a Christ-centered hope must be the foundation of our lives. Hard times come and hard times go, but God's promises are forever. In the end, when this life comes to a close, each of us will be stripped of all earthly wealth and temporal possessions. We will have nothing to hold on to, nothing to grasp, except for the guarantees of God and His Word. So, whether you are facing death or just the next trial, you can be encouraged. Even when all you have is hope, you still have everything you need: namely, the promises of the all-sufficient Savior.

CHAPTER 2

UNLOCKING YOUR SPIRITUAL HOPE CHEST
The Hope God Gives His Family

Praise be to the God and Father of our Lord Jesus Christ!
In his great mercy he has given us new birth into a living hope through
the resurrection of Jesus Christ from the dead, and into an inheritance that can never perish,
spoil or fade—kept in heaven for you.

1 PETER 1:3–4

The value of an inheritance is determined by the net worth of the one who gives it, a fact that was demonstrated to me personally when my great-grandfather passed away. Although he was a man of great character and faith, his material possessions were somewhat meager, meaning that I, as one of many great-grandchildren, received a relatively small inheritance. In fact, I was given only a wrench. Of course, it was a nice wrench, as wrenches go—and I was thankful for the tool—but it was, nonetheless, a rather small heirloom.

I have a friend, on the other hand, whose grandfather is one of the top five hundred wealthiest people in the world—worth hundreds of millions of dollars. Now when that grandfather dies, in terms of worldly possessions, he will surely leave my friend a more extensive inheritance—very possibly millions of dollars, stock options, and a company or two.

I give these examples at the outset simply to demonstrate that, at least financially speaking, an inheritance is only as valuable as the one who gives it. In terms of financial gain and monetary gifts, my friend's grandfather will leave him a much greater inheritance than my great-grandfather left me because his net worth is comparatively much larger.

LOOKING INSIDE
YOUR SPIRITUAL HOPE CHEST

In a similar manner, the Bible speaks of a heavenly inheritance that every Christian can anticipate. In fact, Romans 8:17 declares that we are "heirs of God," meaning that we will receive an endowment from God that is far greater than anything we could ever imagine. Because God's worth is infinite, our spiritual inheritance is worth infinitely more than anything we could receive here on earth. Of course, God's inheritance is a heavenly one rather than an earthly one, but such makes it only more valuable, because it is everlasting and eternally secure. And, just as my great-grandfather died before my inheritance was given to me, God, in the Person of Jesus Christ, died so that we might be "co-heirs with Christ" in receiving our reward as the children of God.

Discussion concerning the believer's spiritual inheritance is not limited only to Romans 8:17. In fact, the Christian's inheritance—a God-guaranteed hope chest filled with divine assurances—is found throughout the New Testament (Ephesians 3:6; Titus 3:7; 1 Peter 1:3–4, 7). Here is a sampling of the promises that our heavenly inheritance includes:

- The promise of Christ's return (Philippians 3:20; 1 Thessalonians 4:13–18; Titus 2:11–14).

- The promise of resurrection (Acts 23:6; 1 Corinthians 15:20–23; Philippians 3:10–11; Revelation 2:11).

- The promise of being made totally righteous (Galatians 5:5; 2 Timothy 4:8; Hebrews 11:7; Revelation 3:5, 12).

- The promise of everlasting life (John 3:16; 1 Corinthians 9:25; James 1:12; 1 John 2:17).

- The promise of heavenly reward (2 Corinthians 5:10; Ephesians 6:8; Colossians 3:24; Revelation 22:12).

- The promise of eternal rest (Hebrews 4:1–11; Revelation 14:13).

- The promise of a new heaven and earth (2 Peter 3:13; Revelation 21:1–2).

These are only some of the absolute guarantees that we, as Christians, can eagerly anticipate and confidently embrace! Of course, the idea of an inheritance primarily points to life after death. However, being an heir means that you are part of God's family. And, being God's child means that He has given you promises for this life, as well. The Bible associates these promises, too, with the concept of hope. So, they are also part of our spiritual hope chest.

- The promise that we can trust God in every situation (Psalm 9:10, 56:3; Nahum 1:7).

- The promise that we cannot lose our salvation (Ephesians 1:13–14; 2 Corinthians 1:22, 5:5).

- The promise that God will continue to grow us spiritually (Romans 5:3–5, 8:28).

- The promise of God's protection (Psalm 25:20–21; 2 Corinthians 1:10–11).

- The promise of God's provision (Jeremiah 14:22; 1 Timothy 5:5).

- The promise that we can find true satisfaction in God (Psalm 62:5; 1 Timothy 6:17).

- The promise of every spiritual blessing in Christ (Ephesians 1:3; Romans 5:1–2).

As an heir of God, we receive infinite benefits for both this life and the next. Hope is not limited only to what comes after death. Rather, our hope chest is brimming with promises for the present as well, given by God Himself, to those who are part of His family.

HOW DO I KNOW THAT I'M PART OF THE FAMILY?

Before we begin an in-depth study of hope, we must each ask ourselves a crucial question: How do I know that I'm an heir of God? After all, only true members of God's family can look forward to opening the hope chest He offers (Romans 8:17). So how can you know for certain whether you are part of that family—an heir? Thankfully, the apostle Paul tells us in the verses preceding Romans 8:17.

1. True children of God recognize that they are sinners (Romans 7:18–25). The book of Romans begins by contrasting mankind's utter rebellion (in chapters 1–3) with God's justifying grace (in chapters 4–6). By chapter 7, Paul speaks plainly about the fact that, of his own accord, he was nothing but a lawbreaker, a sinner. For this reason, he says, "I know that nothing good lives in me, that is, in my sinful nature. For I have the desire to do what is good, but I cannot carry it out" (Romans 7:18). As great a man as he was, Paul knew that in himself there was no inherent goodness or righteousness. He was guilty before a holy God, and he had nothing of his own accord to offer. In realizing this, he cries out, "What a wretched man I am! Who will rescue me from this body of death?" (Romans 7:24).

Paul understood what many in his day did not—that God is not impressed with self-righteousness (see Romans 2:1–11). In fact, in Romans 3:23, he ascribes the description "sinner" to every single human being who has ever lived (with the exception of Christ, of course). All of our efforts to please God "fall short of the glory of God," failing to meet His standard and coming under His judgment. Knowing this, Paul recognizes his sinfulness, understanding that he must trust God for salvation, rather than relying on himself.

2. **True children of God have placed their faith in Christ (Romans 8:1–4).** In contrast to his description of personal spiritual bankruptcy, Paul finds overwhelming joy and exhilaration in the fact that "there is now no condemnation for those who are in Christ Jesus" (Romans 8:1). Being by nature rebellious lawbreakers, all men are worthy of eternal punishment in hell. Yet, God sent His Son, Jesus Christ, to die on the cross as a sin offering, thereby paying the penalty for sin once and for all (see Romans 8:3). In fact, through Jesus' death on the cross, He made it possible for the lawless enemies of God to become His friends (Romans 5:8–10). And, by rising from the dead, Christ proved both that God had accepted His sacrifice and that death had been conquered.

Paul later says, in Romans 10:9–10, that putting one's trust and confidence in Christ's death and resurrection is essential to salvation:

If you confess with your mouth, "Jesus is Lord," and
believe in your heart that God raised him from the dead,
you will be saved. For it is with your heart that you

> *believe and are justified, and it is with your mouth that*
> *you confess and are saved.*

It is this type of faith that characterizes true children of God. Having put their faith in Christ, they recognize that He not only took the penalty they deserved but also gave them His righteousness "in order that the righteous requirements of the law might be fully met" (Romans 8:4).

3. True children of God walk in the Spirit (Romans 8:5–14). Paul continues his description of God's family, noting that true spiritual children demonstrate a change in lifestyle. In other words, belief that God exists is not enough for salvation (James 2:19). God's children are to live lives of repentance, characterized by a change from things sinful to things sanctified.

With this in mind, Paul argues that those who are "in Christ" are those who "do not live according to the sinful nature but according to the Spirit" (Romans 8:4). They are controlled by the Holy Spirit rather than the impulses of sin. In fact, if a person's actions do not correspond with Christ's commandments, it calls into question that person's salvation (v. 9). After all, the apostle clearly states: "Those controlled by the sinful nature cannot please God" (v. 8).

Does this mean that believers are somehow saved by their works? Is Paul saying that faith in Christ, alone, is not enough for entrance into God's family? Certainly not. In fact, Paul just made it clear at the end of Romans 7 that self-righteous works cannot save. So what is Paul saying? The apostle wants to make it clear that *although good works cannot save, those who are saved will produce good works*. In other words, doing righteous activities will not get a person into God's family, but once a part of God's family—through grace alone by faith in Christ alone—righteousness will become the resulting pattern of a Christian's life. In contrast to children of the world, true children of God act like children of God, eliminating sin from their lives (see

Romans 8:13) and pursuing holiness. No wonder Paul says that only "those who are led by the Spirit of God are sons of God" (v. 14).

4. True children are assured by the Spirit (Romans 8:15–16). After describing how God's true children live, Paul reiterates that because believers have received the Holy Spirit, they are now sons of God. They have received the Spirit of adoption (Romans 8:15), meaning that they no longer need to fear, because the God who was once their Judge is now their Father and Friend. As His children, believers may rejoice in the fact that condemnation has been removed (see Romans 8:1).

Paul says, "the Spirit himself testifies with our spirit that we are God's children" (v. 16), which means the Holy Spirit confirms our identity as members of God's family, giving us assurance of our salvation. Of course, our authentication does not come as an audible voice or a letter from heaven. It comes as a result of the transformed life that believers are now able to live, free from sin by the power of the Spirit (see Romans 8:2). In other words, assurance comes through Spirit-led obedience, as the Holy Spirit confirms through our actions what is true in our hearts.

PUTTING IT ALL TOGETHER

If you are not sure whether you really are part of God's family, take a moment to assess your spiritual condition. Do you recognize that you are a sinner before a righteous God, unable in and of yourself to please Him, and therefore worthy of eternal hell? Have you placed your faith completely in the life, death, and resurrection of Jesus Christ for your salvation, realizing that eternal life is only possible through Him? (See John 14:6.) Are you living a life consistent with the commands that Christ has given in Scripture, realizing that although such actions do not save, they do confirm whether your life has been transformed?

If you cannot honestly answer yes to these three questions, maybe now is the time to become a member of God's family. After all, Christ says that "whoever comes to me I will never drive away" (John 6:37). Ask God to forgive your sins through Christ, believe that He alone is the key to salvation, and commit to follow Him with your life—it's that simple. In the end, without Christ the promises discussed in this book will do you no good. They are only promised to heirs—and heirs are those who are part of the family.

THE JOY OF BEING AN HEIR OF GOD

If you know that you are part of God's family, that fact should cause you to rejoice greatly. Instead of one day facing condemnation, you get to look forward to your spiritual inheritance. Because Christ died for you, you have been adopted into God's family!

As you think about your spiritual hope chest, God wants the inheritance He's promised you to change your perspective. He wants you to be overwhelmed and overjoyed with what He has planned for you as His child, both for this life and the next. Some of these promises may be new to you; others may be well established in your thinking. No matter how familiar or new, when people search God's Word for His guarantees, they will inevitably encounter the comforting, rejuvenating, and motivating power of the hope of Scripture. So, as you read the rest of this book, I echo Paul's words to the Ephesians, "I pray also that the eyes of your heart may be enlightened in order that you may know the hope to which he has called you, the riches of his glorious inheritance in the saints" (Ephesians 1:18).

CHAPTER 3

WHEN GOD GIVES HIS WORD:

Hope Is a Promise (Part 1)

*Paul, a servant of God and an apostle of Jesus Christ for the faith of
God's elect and the knowledge of the truth that leads to godliness—
a faith and knowledge resting on the hope of eternal life,
which God, who does not lie, promised before the beginning of time.*

TITUS 1:1–2

Our society is plagued with broken promises. They can be found in the family, at school, and in the workplace. They are present in the government—often in the campaign pledges of one or more aspiring candidates. Sometimes they even come to our very own mailboxes—with false assurances of instant winnings and millions upon millions of dollars.

Saying one thing but never following through has become an American epidemic. In fact, according to the book *The Day Americans Told the Truth*, 86 percent of Americans routinely lie to parents, 75 percent to friends, 73 percent to siblings, and 69 percent to spouses. As a result, our nation has developed a healthy sense of skepticism. Those who believe everything everyone tells them are derided as gullible fools. After all, if it sounds too good to be true, it probably is. Promises are easily made, says our socity, but don't get your hopes up because you'll only be disappointed.

GOD DOESN'T MAKE EMPTY PROMISES

The Bible, on the other hand, invites you to get your hopes up. Of course, Scripture is very specific as to what true hope includes. Hoping for instant riches to land in your mailbox is probably foolhardy. Hoping in the promises of God, however, is nothing less than the essence of faith. Unlike the broken and empty promises of greedy politicians, negligent parents, or shady publicity stunts, God's Word never fails. In fact, the Bible says it lasts forever (Psalm 119:52). But how do you know that you can trust God completely? What guarantees do you have that God's promises are legitimate?

Thankfully, God's Word gives us many reasons to take solace in His promises. Over and over again the Scripture commands us and compels us to trust God, both for the present and the future. The assurances that comprise our hope are not too good to be true—and they are infinitely better than any earthly guarantee. They are certainties upon which we can build our lives and our eternities. They can be trusted because they come from a God who can be trusted. In this chapter and the next, we will consider five reasons Christians can confidently hope in God:

1. HIS PERSON: You Can Hope in God Because of Who He Is. First, you can hope in God's promises because He is absolutely trustworthy—His Word can be trusted because He can be trusted. God's personality backs up the reliability of everything He says. Unlike the stereotypical used-car salesman, God's character does not contradict His promises. As a result, we can be confident that every assurance He makes will come to pass exactly as foretold, down to the smallest detail. But what is it about God's person that makes

Him so trustworthy? In order to answer this question, at least three divine attributes must be considered:

a. *God is wise.* Believers can hope in God, first of all, because He is perfectly wise. In fact, Psalm 147:5 notes that His understanding is infinite. And Paul, in Romans 11:33–34, exclaims, "Oh, the depth of the riches of the wisdom and knowledge of God! How unsearchable his judgments, and his paths beyond tracing out!" He needs no additional advice or help because He already possesses infinite understanding. God knows every situation, circumstance, and possibility in complete detail—and He knows how to handle each one perfectly.

As Christians, we can place our confidence fully in God's decisions because He knows exactly what He's doing. Our response to God's perfect wisdom, then, must be to trust in Him rather than in ourselves or anything else. Even Solomon, the wisest of men, advised, "Trust in the LORD with all your heart and lean not on your own understanding" (Proverbs 3:5).

b. *God is righteous.* Along with God's wisdom, His perfect righteousness also allows us to hope in Him completely. The Bible is clear: God is absolutely holy, without sin, and morally perfect in every way (see Daniel 9:14; 1 John 1:5). In fact, God's holiness is a motivation for our own righteous living. Peter, quoting from Leviticus, urges his readers, "But just as he who called you is holy, so be holy in all you do; for it is written: 'Be holy, because I am holy'" (1 Peter 1:15–16).

So how does God's righteousness fit in with His trustworthiness? The answer is simple: Because lying is a sin (Proverbs 6:16–17, 12:22), God's righteousness does not allow Him to have any part in it—God cannot lie because God cannot sin. His righteousness means that He will never act in any way that compromises or contradicts His own character. Unlike a crooked politician who says one thing but means another, our holy God always means exactly what He says. He can be trusted because He is pure, and breaking His Word would violate His character.

c. *God is unchanging.* Not only is God perfectly wise and perfectly righteous, but His character never changes. Psalm 102:26–27, directed to God, says, "They will perish, but you remain; they will all wear out like a garment. Like clothing you will change them and they will be discarded. But you remain the same, and your years will never end." James 1:17 reiterates this point, noting that in God there is no shifting of shadows. Hebrews 13:8 says, "Jesus Christ is the same yesterday and today and forever." Despite the turmoil or transition of those on this earth, God's character remains constant.

Regarding hope, God's immutable nature means that He's not going to suddenly change His mind about previous promises. He won't arbitrarily decide that salvation is no longer found in Christ or that eternal life is no longer available. After all, the God in whom we first put our hope is still the same God now. We can cling tightly to the hope God has given because an unchanging God can only make unchanging promises.

God's person—specifically, His wisdom, righteousness, and unchanging nature—allows us to trust Him because of who He is. His words are certain because His character is certain. As Hebrews 6:18 puts it: "It is impossible for God to lie."

2. HIS POWER: You Can Hope in God Because He Is in Control. A second reason to hope in God, beyond His dependable character, is His perfect power. Again, the Bible is very clear—God is in control of everything at every moment of every day. His power is infinite, knowing no viable rivals or exclusions. God alone is King and He is King over all. Here are some categories over which God wields absolute authority:

- God is sovereign over evil, sin, Satan, and demons (Job 1:12, 2:6; Lamentations 3:38; Luke 5:21, 8:31, 22:31; Revelation 20:10–15).

- God is sovereign over the governments and militaries of

every nation (2 Chronicles 20:6; Psalm 20:7; Proverbs 21:1; Romans 13:2; John 19:11).

- God is sovereign over nature, including natural disasters (Psalm 50:10, 107:29; Amos 4:7; Nahum 1:3–6; Matthew 5:45; Luke 8:24).

- God is sovereign over sickness and disease (Exodus 15:26; Deuteronomy 32:39; 2 Kings 20:5; Matthew 4:23; Mark 6:56; John 9:1–3; Acts 4:29–30).

- God is sovereign over other people and their choices (Exodus 8:15; Proverbs 21:1; Acts 13:48; Romans 9:17–18).

- God is sovereign over our own personal plans (Proverbs 16:9, 19:21; James 4:13–15).

- God is sovereign over chance and fate (Proverbs 16:33; Job 20:29, 21:17).

- God is sovereign over everything in the universe (Psalm 115:3, 135:6; Ephesians 1:11).

Is there anything in the universe outside of God's control? No! In fact, every potential danger we might face in life is under the supervision of an all-powerful God. Of course, this does not excuse our own responsibility—such as resisting temptation (James 4:7) or being properly prepared (Nehemiah 4:9). However, it does mean that we can put our hope fully in God and His guarantees. Because He is in control of all things, no circumstance, setting, or individual exists or acts without God's permission. So, when He promises to save us, we can be confident that nothing "will be able to separate us from the love of God that is in Christ Jesus our Lord" (Romans 8:39). In the end, then, nothing can thwart God's promises because, quite simply, His power won't allow it (see John 10:28–29).

What comfort there is in knowing that nothing in this universe is greater than our God! Even the most powerful natural and man-made forces are subject to His reign. What comes to your mind when you think of great power? Maybe it's the military might of the nation in which you live. The United States military alone has 1.4 million soldiers in active duty, with personnel in more than 130 countries. Maybe you think of an earthquake or a volcano. Mount St. Helens, for example, was triggered by a 5.1 magnitude earthquake, shooting fire and lava fifteen miles into the air. Maybe you think of heavy winds or a devastating thunderstorm, realizing that while individual lightning bolts average two to three miles long with a current of one hundred million volts, some can stretch up to seventy-five miles in length.

You might think of the sea and the creatures that live there. After all, the ocean covers 71 percent of the earth's surface, its deepest point being almost seven miles down. Or maybe your thoughts turn to outer space, where the sun's volume alone could fit 1.3 million earths—and there are innumerable other stars that are larger than the sun. You may even contemplate spiritual forces, Satan and his minions, and the power they wield. Yet, no matter what you can think of or even imagine, God is more powerful still. He is the One who names and numbers the stars (Psalm 147:4), who regards the nations as a speck of dust (Isaiah 40:15), who quiets the seas with a word (Job 26:12; Matthew 8:26), and who will one day win the final victory (1 Corinthians 15:20–28). Clearly, if God is our Refuge and Strength, we have nothing to fear.

PROMISES TO BUILD YOUR LIFE ON

God's righteous character and His infinite power are two incredible reasons that we can believe the promises He's given us. He is always just, and He is always in control. There is nothing that can happen to us that He does not allow. And there is no one who can separate us from His love (Romans 8:38–39). It is important to understand that our heavenly hope chest is guaranteed by a trustworthy God. He *will* do what He says because He cannot contradict Himself (Psalm 145:13; Titus 1:2). And He *can* do what He promises because He has the power to do whatever He pleases (Psalm 115:3).

In the next chapter, we will continue to survey God's trustworthiness. Unless God can be believed, His promises are meaningless; unless He is telling the truth, our hope is groundless. On the flip side, because He can be trusted, we can base our eternities on the truths of His Word.

CHAPTER 4

A God You Can Trust
Hope Is a Promise (Part 2)

> *Let us hold unswervingly to the hope we profess,*
> *for he who promised is faithful.*
>
> HEBREWS 10:23

Things are not always what they seem, a fact clearly evidenced by the following illustration from *Reader's Digest*:

> As a prospective Harvard student, I was taking a campus tour when the guide stopped before a statue in Harvard Yard. On the pedestal was this inscription: "John Harvard, Founder, 1638."
>
> The guide informed us that this was known as "the statue of the three lies."
>
> First of all, the artist commissioned to sculpture it could not find a clear picture of John Harvard after which to model his work, so he just chose a picture of a respectable-looking gentleman from the proper era.
>
> Second, John Harvard was not the founder of

*Harvard University. He was simply a substantial con-
tributor to the college in its early days.*

*Third, the date on the statue's base represents not
the date of John Harvard's death, as might be supposed,
but the year he donated his library and half his fortune
to the college.*

*The irony lies in that on the side of the statue is the
Harvard emblem emblazoned with the school's motto:
Veritas [or "Truth"].[1]*

Like the Harvard motto, the Bible also claims the title "Truth."
Yet, unlike the statue of John Harvard, the Bible does not give us a
false impression of who God is. In fact, the picture we have of Him
in Scripture is not make-believe, it is His own self-portrait. The
claims that He makes are not stretched or misleading, they are
absolutely certain. His attributes, as described by His Word, are not
human inventions or mythical enhancements, they are the essence of
who He really is. Therefore, when He says that His promises are
true, we can be confident to believe them.

As we saw in chapter 3, God's character is absolutely trustworthy, and His power means He is in total control. In other words, we
can hope in God not only for who He is, but also for what He can
do. As we continue to study our faithful God, we will consider three
more reasons that you can hope in Him.

**3. HIS PLAN: You Can Hope in God Because He Knows
Exactly What He's Doing.** If God was merely all powerful, haphazardly wielding brute force at random spurts throughout the universe,
we might have reason to be frightened. But, as we have seen, God is
not only all-powerful, He is also all-wise. This means He has a perfect
plan that He is faithfully working out in history (Isaiah 25:1). In
Isaiah 46:10 God says, "I make known the end from the beginning,
from ancient times, what is still to come. I say: My purpose will stand,

and I will do all that I please." Psalm 33:11 echoes, "The plans of the LORD stand firm forever, the purposes of his heart through all generations." But what does God's plan include? The answer comes in at least two parts.

a. *God's plan mandates that He receive maximum glory.* Scripture says everyone and everything was created by God to bring Him glory and praise (Isaiah 43:7; 1 Chronicles 16:2, 29:11; Psalm 8:1, 19:1; Ezekiel 43:2; 1 Corinthians 10:31). In fact, the primary reason God saved us was to further His reputation as a gracious God—that we would praise Him for His mercy (Romans 9:15–24). God's passion for His own glory is not only right but should be our greatest passion, as well. After all, He is the only One in the universe worthy of such honor and praise.

Regarding hope, God's passion for His own reputation guarantees that He will keep the promises He has made to His children. After all, were He to fail in keeping His word, His name would be tarnished and His glory would suffer. We can trust that God will keep His promises, not on account of our good works, but rather because His name is at stake (see Exodus 32:9–14). For the sake of His glory, He will certainly follow through on the promises He's made us.

b. *God's plan mandates that believers receive maximum good.* In perfect conjunction with His glory, God's plan also includes the well-being of His people. The apostle Paul declares that "in all things God works for the good of those who love him, who have been called according to his purpose" (Romans 8:28). In other words, God uses every circumstance and every person in our lives for our spiritual betterment—to make us more like Christ. Granted, the good sometimes comes in the form of discipline (Hebrews 12:10) or trials (James 1:2–3). Yet, even these are for our good—that through repentance or endurance we would grow stronger in our faith. Of course, God's definition of good does not necessarily include the temporal pleasures and wealth we so often desire. Rather, He defines it in terms of our spiritual growth and eternal benefit.

In His perfect wisdom, God's plan merges both His passion for His glory and His concern for our good. Consequently, we find our greatest joy and satisfaction (or good) when we are pursuing Him—and His glory—most vigorously. And vice versa. As John Piper says, "God is most glorified in us, when we are most satisfied in Him."[2]

Because God's plan includes our good, we can rest confidently in His promises to us. Not only are the promises He makes unbreakable, because His reputation is at stake, but they are also beneficial. They can be trusted because they were made with our best interest in mind.

4. HIS PAST RECORD: You Can Hope in God Because He's Been Faithful Before. Another reason we can embrace the hope God offers is because He has never broken a promise. His track record is perfect. He has always kept His Word in the past, just as He will continue to do so in the future. The biblical record is clear: God is impeccably faithful.

For example, in Psalm 100:5, the writer says, "For the LORD is good and his love endures forever; his faithfulness continues through all generations." Earlier in Psalms, Asaph overcomes his despair by remembering "the deeds of the LORD; yes, I will remember your miracles of long ago" (Psalm 77:11). And 1 Chronicles 16:15 notes that God "remembers his covenant forever, the word he commanded, for a thousand generations." Ethan, in discussing God's promises to David, announces, "I will sing of the LORD's great love forever; with my mouth I will make your faithfulness known through all generations" (Psalm 89:1). And Psalm 119:90, speaking to God, echoes: "Your faithfulness continues through all generations."

God's faithfulness is not just an abstract part of who He is.

Rather, it is an attribute that has been proven throughout history time and time again. As Christians, by remembering God's provision and protection in the past, we can hope expectantly in Him for the present and the future. Even in the midst of trials and suffering, we can be confident that He who was faithful before is still "faithful in all he does" (Psalm 33:4).

5. HIS PARENTAL CARE: You Can Hope in God Because He Loves You. A final reason to hope in God is found in the love He has for His children. In the Old Testament, God demonstrated His love to Israel again and again (Deuteronomy 23:5; Exodus 34:6–7). Over twenty-five times, in Psalms alone, is God's love called "unfailing" (Psalm 6:4, 21:7, and 90:14, to name a few). We can both "trust in" (Psalm 13:5) and "be glad and rejoice in" (Psalm 31:7) the love of God. Solomon, in 2 Chronicles 6:14, refers to God's promises as covenants of love (see also Nehemiah 1:5). Even Jeremiah, after Jerusalem's destruction, finds comfort in "the Lord's unfailing love" (Lamentations 3:32).

God's great love for His children is found in the New Testament, as well. After all, it was on account of His love for the world that God gave His Son in the first place (John 3:16; Ephesians 2:4; Titus 3:4; 1 John 4:19). Christ's death was the ultimate proof: "But God demonstrates his own love for us in this: While we were still sinners, Christ died for us" (Romans 5:8). It was out of His love that He predestined us to salvation (Ephesians 1:4–5; 1 Thessalonians 4:9). Even in disciplining us, it is God's love, not His wrath, that motivates His hand (Hebrews 12:6).

Regarding hope, 1 Corinthians 13:8 clearly states that "love never fails." If God who is love (1 John 4:8) loves us (1 John 4:10), then we can be confident that He will never let us down (Romans 8:38–39). With Paul we can confidently assert that "hope does not disappoint us, because God has poured out his love into our hearts by the Holy

Spirit, whom he has given us" (Romans 5:5). We can cling to God's promises because He guarantees them as a loving Father.

PUTTING IT ALL TOGETHER

As we have seen, hoping in God is synonymous with trusting Him for the promises He has given us as His children. In considering this truth, I can't help imagining the little boy who looks down at his father, willing to jump from what seems to be an enormous height, because he is confident that his daddy will catch him. A plunge he would never otherwise take, the child leaps eagerly into the air, unafraid of gravity's pull or the firm earth below. There is nothing to fear; his daddy promised to catch him and he's never been dropped before.

Life is often like that jump. There is an element of uncertainty and unknown. The pitfalls and drop-offs are very real and very dangerous. Yet, as God's children, we have no reason to worry or cower, our heavenly Father will catch us. Whether we face temporary trials or the final reality of death, we need not be afraid. God is there with us, and He'll be there on the other side, as well.

Like that young boy, we have no reason not to trust our Father. After all, He is a promise-keeping God who does not take back His words (Isaiah 31:2). We can hope in Him because of who He is (His Person), because of what He can do (His power), because of what He is doing (His plan), because of what He has already done (His past record), and because of how much He loves those who belong to Him (His parental care).

So, when God offers us hope, it is much more than just a desired possibility. The promises God has made to us are certain. They will not be foiled, because God is in total control. They will not be let-downs, because they involve our utmost good. And, finally, they will not be broken, because God keeps His Word. Biblical hope is true hope. It can be embraced with confidence, because of the God who guarantees it: "I am the LORD; those who hope in me will not be disappointed" (Isaiah 49:23). Our response, as Hebrews 10:23 urges, should be to "hold unswervingly to the hope we profess, for he who promised is faithful."

CHAPTER 5

THE DAY HOPE DIED FOR YOU:

Hope Is a Person

" Here is my servant whom I have chosen, the one I love, in whom I delight;

I will put my Spirit on him, and he will proclaim justice to the nations.

He will not quarrel or cry out; no one will hear his voice in the streets.

A bruised reed he will not break, and a smoldering wick he will not snuff out, till he leads justice to victory.

In his name the nations will put their hope. "

MATTHEW 12:18–21

Imagine yourself at Calvary—a Jew drawn to the site solely out of curiosity. The angry mob around you grows larger, as do the thick, dark clouds on the horizon. Mixed with the cries of the restless crowd, both of ridicule and pity, the air's cold chill sends shivers down your spine. You can't help noticing the rocky, barren landscape—fitting for a place called "The Skull."

All eyes are focused on the second of three Roman crosses, hastily pounded into the dusty turf. On it hangs a man; the sign above His head reads, "King of the Jews." As you move a little closer to Him you notice that His muscular frame is bent and sagging. Blood pours from His back and from His thorn-lacerated brow. He is in agony; His breaths are slow and labored; His face swollen and discolored. "Some king!" shouts an angry man standing nearby.

You glance down to the people surrounding the cross. On one side stand the victim's friends and family. They are weeping and distraught—forced to keep their distance by a cohort of Roman soldiers. On the other side are His enemies—mostly religious leaders and a few bystanders caught up in the moment. "You saved others, save Yourself!" they taunt. His only response: "Father, forgive them; for they know not what they do" (Luke 23:34 KJV).

Moments turn from minutes into hours as the sky grows increasingly dark and gloomy. Many begin to leave for their homes knowing that the Passover celebration will soon be under way. Yet even as those around you turn to go, a loud cry constrains them to look back. It is Jesus. "Father, into your hands I commit my spirit" (Luke 23:46). Immediately, His body goes limp. The crowd goes simultaneously silent. Slowly whispers ripple through the multitude. "I think He's dead," says someone close to you. "I guess He wasn't everything we'd hoped He would be."

You nod slowly, not realizing that He had to die to conquer sin and that He would rise again to conquer death. In fact, it's not until several weeks later, at Pentecost, that you hear the whole story from Jesus' zealous disciples: Jesus Christ is the true Messiah, the Hope of Israel. His death was a necessary sacrifice for sin, His resurrection a proof that God was pleased with His payment. Only now do you begin to understand that the day you stood on Golgotha involved something infinitely more significant than just another execution. It was the day your sins were paid for—the day Hope died for you.

JESUS CHRIST, OUR HOPE

Some thirty years after His birth in Bethlehem, Jesus Christ was murdered by those He came to save. Through both His life and His death, Jesus changed history forever. The calendar, the Roman empire, the lives of His followers—all irrevocably altered as a result of His ministry. Almost everyone today has at least heard His name, and most know a little bit about Him.

It is not surprising, then, to discover a plethora of different opinions about who Jesus was and why He came. Some argue that He was simply a good man whose teachings have moral value. Others disagree, perhaps considering Him a fanatic. A few do not even think He lived at all. The Bible, however, argues that Jesus was a true historical figure who literally lived and died (1 John 4:2–3). His claims were accurate and His miracles real. Anything less means that Jesus was a fraud and our hope in Him is worthless (1 Corinthians 15:17). With this in mind, the biblical picture of Jesus must be understood and embraced if we are to fully appreciate the One whom Paul calls "our hope" (1 Timothy 1:1). Here are four reasons you can hope in Christ:

1. You Can Hope in Christ Because He Is Both God and Man. The Bible says Jesus is both 100 percent divine and 100 percent human. While the details of this union are beyond human comprehension, the Bible is clear that both truths are correct—Jesus Christ is, at the same time, both God and man.

Of these two truths, Jesus' deity is probably the most debated. God's Word, however, makes the issue black and white. For example, Jesus is called God (John 1:1, 18; Titus 2:13; Hebrews 1:8; 1 John 5:20) and also Lord—the New Testament equivalent of *Yahweh*—(Acts 10:36; 2 Peter 3:2). Claiming equality with God the Father (John 5:18, 10:28–36, 19:7), Jesus demonstrated His divine nature through His infinite knowledge (John 2:24–25, 6:64; Colossians 2:3) and supernatural power (Philippians 3:20–21). Morally, He was absolutely perfect (Luke 1:35; Acts 3:14; 2 Timothy 4:8; Revelation 3:7)—a character trait belonging only to God (compare Deuteronomy

32:4 with Acts 3:23). In ministry, He worked as only God could work: forgiving sins (Mark 2:5–12; Colossians 3:13), offering eternal life (John 10:28), pledging to build His church (Matthew 16:18), demonstrating authority over angels and demons (Matthew 13:41; Mark 1:25; Luke 8:30–31), and even promising to answer prayer (John 14:14). It is no surprise, then, that those around Him knew exactly who He was claiming to be (John 1:34, 10:33; Mark 14:28, 15:39)—namely, the only One worthy of their worship (Matthew 4:10, 14:33, 15:25, 28:9).

Regarding His humanity, the Bible is equally clear. Not only did He have an ancestry (Matthew 1:1–18; Luke 3:23–38; Mark 6:3) and a human birth (Matthew 1:25; Luke 1:26–35), He also grew up as a normal human child (Luke 2:40). He experienced the full spectrum of human emotions and experiences: hunger (Luke 4:2), thirst (John 4:7), fatigue (Mark 4:38), and sorrow (John 11:35). His body bled when pierced (John 19:34), and bruised when beaten (Matthew 26:67; Mark 14:65). To all who saw Him, His appearance was that of an actual, physical human being. While He truly was the Son of God, He was equally the Son of Man (Matthew 16:13, 16; John 1:49–51, 6:27, 12:34).

The fact that Christ is both God and man is intrinsically intertwined with the believer's hope. After all, because Jesus is God, He could perfectly meet God's righteous standard as a sacrifice for our sin. And, because Jesus is also completely human, He can wholly sympathize with those He came to save. As both, He is the perfect Mediator—able to interact with God as God and with man as a man. Although He is completely righteous and infinitely capable, the Person of Hope is not distant, cold, or uncaring. We can hope in Him because as God, He is powerful enough to save, and as man, He knows exactly what we need.

2. You Can Hope in Jesus Christ Because He Died and Rose Again. A second reason to hope in Christ is found in His death and resurrection. Having lived an absolutely perfect life (Hebrews 4:15; 1 John 2:1), He sacrificed Himself as the spotless Lamb of God (1 Peter 1:19). Although He never sinned, He was crucified for the sins of those He came to save (see Luke 19:10; Mark 10:45); and because the penalty for sin is death (Romans 6:23), Jesus had to die in order to pay sin's price (2 Corinthians 5:21; 1 Peter 2:24). Paul makes this clear in Romans 5:8–9: "But God demonstrates his own love for us in this: While we were still sinners, Christ died for us. Since we have now been justified by his blood, how much more shall we be saved from God's wrath through him!" This incredible truth is echoed in 1 Peter 3:18: "For Christ died for sins once for all, the righteous for the unrighteous, to bring you to God."

It is important to realize that sin's penalty could only have been paid through Christ's death. Human effort can never save (Isaiah 64:6), nor will keeping God's law (Galatians 2:21). Salvation is only available through Jesus (John 14:6), because only He could satisfy God's judgment (Isaiah 53:9; Romans 8:3–4). His death is at the very heart of our hope because it is the basis for our eternal life. Because Christ died, we live (1 Thessalonians 5:10).

But Christ did not just die. No, the Bible also argues that He conquered death by rising again three days later (Matthew 28:5–6; Acts 7:54–56; 1 Corinthians 15:3–4). In His resurrection, Jesus proved that God had accepted His sacrifice and that He truly was the Savior (Acts 13:34–38). As Romans 1:4 proclaims, Jesus Christ "was declared with power to be the Son of God by his resurrection from the dead." That means we can be confident that Jesus is who He claimed to be because God raised Him from the grave. Also, as His followers, we can hope in our own future resurrection because He has already been raised (1 Corinthians 6:14).

3. You Can Hope in Jesus Christ Because He Is Currently in Heaven. So where did Christ go after His resurrection? Well, the Bible says that after spending a short time on earth, He ascended to

heaven, where He is currently. Having been "exalted to the right hand of God" (Acts 2:33), He now intercedes on behalf of believers before His Father (1 John 2:1; Hebrews 9:24), acting as the Christian's High Priest (Hebrews 8:1–2, 10:12) while also working in His church through the Holy Spirit (John 16:5–7). Yet, He is not planning to stay in heaven forever. He plans on returning to earth a second time—not as the Savior, but as the Judge (Acts 17:31; 2 Thessalonians 1:6–10). In fact, Christ's ascension foreshadows His return, the way He went up is the way He'll come back down (Acts 1:11).

Because Christ went up to heaven and is currently there, we can be certain that we will go to be with Him when we die (2 Corinthians 5:8). Also, we can confidently hope in His return and His future reign—that one day He will rescue those who are His while righting the injustices of our fallen world. Although He is now in heaven, He is nonetheless very much alive, very much God, and very much intent on returning to deliver the righteous and to judge sinners.

4. You Can Hope in Christ Because He Fulfilled God's Promise. As early as Genesis 3:15, only moments after history's first sin, God indicated He would send Someone to save our fallen race. Later in Genesis, Jacob foreshadowed the coming Savior on his deathbed (Genesis 49:10–11). Even the Old Testament sacrificial system pointed to the ultimate Sacrifice (Hebrews 10:1–10).

The prophet Isaiah spoke of His suffering (Isaiah 52:13–53:12) as did the psalmist (Psalm 22:1–31). Yet, they also foresaw His greatness—His delivering power and rule (Psalm 2:9; Isaiah 42:1–4). These expectations were heightened by the minor prophets, who declared His kingdom to be a coming reality (Amos 9:11–15; Zephaniah 3:14–20; Zechariah 14:16–21). Needless to say, by the time of Jesus' birth, Israel was eagerly anticipating the Messiah (Luke 2:25–38).

Jesus came, then, as a fulfillment of Old Testament prophecy. God had promised that He would send a Savior, and Jesus was that promised One (Acts 13:32–33). Although only some of the many

Old Testament prophecies were fulfilled in Christ's first coming, those that were fulfilled all came to pass literally and completely. As a result, we can be confident that the other biblical promises about the Messiah will also be perfectly fulfilled when Christ returns. As the promised Savior of God, Jesus Christ is proof that God always does exactly what He says He will do. For this reason, Paul saw Jesus as the "hope of Israel" (Acts 28:20), the One who fulfilled God's Old Testament guarantees (Acts 26:6–7).

Our Hope for Today and Tomorrow

God's Word makes no apologies in asserting that true hope is only found in and through Jesus Christ. After all, Jesus Himself says, "I am the way and the truth and the life. No one comes to the Father except through me" (John 14:6). He alone offers eternal life (John 4:14) and perfect rest for the soul (Matthew 11:29). Only He can give permanent satisfaction (John 6:35), perfect guidance (John 8:12), and absolute protection (John 10:7–14). It is solely through His work on the cross that sinners can be made right before the heavenly Judge (Romans 3:23–24, 6:23). Many may claim the role of savior (Matthew 24:5), but only Jesus Christ is our true Hope. In the end, those who choose to reject the Person of hope will one day find themselves hopeless before a holy God (John 8:24). On the other hand, those who put their hope in Jesus will have nothing to fear (1 John 4:15–18).

While many in this world look frantically for something to hope in, Christians can rest with assurance in the person and work of Jesus Christ. After all, He is God's promised Savior, the fulfillment of God's Word, and the foundation of our futures. Salvation, then, is only found in Him—through the penalty He paid on the day He died for you.

HOMESICK FOR HEAVEN:

Hope Is a Place

But in keeping with his promise we are looking forward to
a new heaven and a new earth, the home of righteousness.

2 PETER 3:13

Some time ago, I attended the funeral of Dr. Charles Smith, one of my Bible professors from college. He had been a teacher for more than fifty years, diligently proclaiming the truth he consistently practiced. His love for life, his passion for Scripture, and his anticipation for eternity were all contagious. Even in death, his faithful Christian testimony stood as an example for those who knew him.

More than thirty years before his death, Dr. Smith penned the words of his own epitaph. They were printed in his funeral program, and they reflect a perspective that few possess—a perspective that was homesick for heaven.

I saw a leaf fall to the ground today. . .
For an entire season it had clung proudly to its place,
gleaming brightly in the summer sun. It had felt its

usefulness and beauty. But when embraced to Autumn's cold breast, its beauty faded; it became shriveled and sere. Still, it clung tenaciously to its accustomed spot on the branch. After much urging by a gentle wind, it wavered between its desire to remain with the known, and the desire to experience the unknown. Finally, it embarked on its new adventure, and sailed happily with the breeze and gently fluttered to join many of its old companions, and to meet many new of brighter hue. When it came to rest, I think I heard it release a sigh of contentment.

I am now in the summer of my life—enjoying my place, feeling of some use and service. When the late Autumn of my life comes, I think I shall be like that leaf I saw fall today. Certainly, I shall hesitate to leave the accustomed. But I know that once the great adventure is begun, I shall sail into eternal contentment.

You who see the leaf of my life fade and fall: Do not mistake that final breath as a groan. It will be a joyful sigh of release into the hands of my Great God, Creator, and Savior.

What an example of faith and confidence—of a truly heavenly mind-set. As Paul said in Philippians 1:21–23, "to die is gain" because "to depart and be with Christ. . .is better by far." Yet we so often cling to the branch of this life as though it is all we have. We don't look forward to heaven because we're too comfortable down here. In practice, we've gladly exchanged our heavenly home for this temporal world.

In contrast to this pervading mind-set, God's Word commands us to store up "treasures in heaven, where moth and rust do not destroy, and where thieves do not break in and steal" (Matthew 6:20). In fact, the Bible gives us at least five reasons to focus on our eternal home—five motivations for why Christians should put their hope in heaven.

1. You Can Hope in Heaven Because Heaven Is a Real Place. In the modern mind-set, heaven is more fairy tale than fact. In an age of academic achievement, scientific advancement, and medical accomplishment, the thought of heaven is often deemed laughable. It's placed in the same category as Area 51, UFOs, and little green men from Mars. Maybe it doesn't really exist, maybe it's just a way of dealing with the pain of loss, or maybe it's nothing more than wishful thinking. C. S. Lewis, in *The Problem of Pain,* responds:

> *We are very shy nowadays of even mentioning Heaven. We are afraid of the jeer about "pie in the sky," and of being told that we are trying to "escape from the duty of making a happy world here and now into dreams of a happy world elsewhere." But either there is "pie in the sky" or there is not. If there is not, then Christianity is false, for this doctrine is woven into its whole fabric. If there is, then this truth, like any other, must be faced, whether it is useful at political meetings or no.[1]*

What many in this world excuse as delusional, Scripture affirms as absolute fact. There is, indeed, "pie in the sky." And, the Bible is very quick to define exactly what heaven is like. It is the dwelling place of God the Father (Psalm 33:13; Matthew 6:9), the dwelling place of Jesus Christ (Hebrews 1:3, 8:1), and the home of saints who have died (Philippians 1:23; 2 Corinthians 5:8). It is a place of holiness (Revelation 4:8), light (Revelation 21:23), worship (Revelation 5:9–14), angelic activity (Matthew 18:10), and perfect peace (Revelation 21:4). In the future, after Christ returns, the delights of heaven will be recreated in a new heaven and earth (Revelation 21:1). Here is where all of God's children, through all of the ages, will enjoy eternity in their resurrected bodies (1 Corinthians 15:40–49). God will set up His throne in the new Jerusalem (Revelation 21:2), death and sin will be no more

(1 Corinthians 15:25–26), and we will worship our King forever and ever (Isaiah 66:22–24).

Never does Scripture suggest that heaven is merely a spiritual façade or an empty motive for religious fervor. Rather, it is an eternal reality, the Christian's true home, the throne room of God Himself. To believe the Bible is to believe in heaven; to trust in Christ is to trust in His promise "to prepare a place for you" (John 14:2–3); to doubt heaven, is to doubt God Himself.

2. You Can Hope in Heaven Because Heaven Is Part of Your Inheritance. Not only is heaven a Bible-backed reality, it is also God's promise to those who are His. After all, what comfort is there in knowing heaven exists if there is no hope of ever getting there? Yet, Scripture plainly teaches that all who belong to Christ also belong in heaven (see Revelation 21:6–7).

An eternal home with God Himself is not only part of our inheritance (2 Peter 3:13), it is also the place where we receive the rest of our inheritance and our eternal reward (Matthew 5:1–16; Colossians 1:5; 1 Peter 1:4). While we will unpack the specific elements of this inheritance in subsequent chapters, the bottom line is that heaven should be something every Christian eagerly anticipates. Why are we so afraid of death? Maybe it is because we are not as homesick for heaven as we should be. After five minutes of heaven, we'll wonder why we tried so hard to avoid arriving there sooner.

D. L. Moody, in his *Anecdotes,* recounts an old legend about a swan and a crane. One day, while the crane was searching for snails, he saw a swan alight on the shore nearby. The crane had never seen another bird like this swan, and after staring curiously for a few moments, the crane asked the swan from where she came.

> *"I come from heaven!" replied the swan.*
> *"And where is heaven?" asked the crane.*
> *"Heaven!" said the swan, "Heaven! Have you never*

heard of heaven?" And the beautiful bird went on to describe the grandeur of the Eternal City. She told of streets of gold, and the gates and walls made of precious stones; of the river of life, pure as crystal, upon whose banks is the tree whose leaves shall be for the healing of the nations. In eloquent terms the swan sought to describe the hosts who live in the other world, but without arousing the slightest interest on the part of the crane.

Finally the crane asked: "Are there any snails there?"

"Snails!" repeated the swan. "No! Of course there are not!"

"Then," said the crane, as it continued its search along the slimy banks of the pool, "you can have your heaven. I want snails!"[2]

Why do so many today, like that crane, spend their time in search of earthly snails? Do they not realize that heavenly grandeur awaits? God offers us eternal treasure; why would we waste our time pursuing what will never last? How quickly we forget that our inheritance is in glory, the dwelling place of God Himself. As Christians, we should live so as to reflect our incredible future.

3. You Can Hope in Heaven Because Heaven Is Where Christ Is. Not only is heaven the Christian's promised inheritance, it is also the home of the Savior Himself. In fact, all of the blessings, glories, and rewards of heaven find their source and culmination in Him. Were there no Lamb, there would be no heavenly promise. Were there no Savior, there would be no salvation. Christ is not only the door into paradise (John 14:6; Revelation 21:27) but also its eternal focal point (Revelation 5:11–14, 19:1–2). Heaven—in its essence—is to be with Christ (Philippians 1:23).

J. I. Packer expresses this perspective when he says:

We know very little about heaven, but I once heard a theologian describe it as "an unknown region with a well-known inhabitant," and there is not a better way to think of it than that.... To those who have learned to love and trust Jesus, the prospect of meeting Him face-to-face and being with Him forever is the hope that keeps us going, no matter what life may throw at us.[3]

Even now, Christ is in heaven preparing a place for us (John 14:2–3), meaning that, because He is our hope, we can hope in the promise of spending eternity with Him (2 Corinthians 5:8; Philippians 1:23; 1 Peter 3:22).

4. You Can Hope in Heaven Because Heaven Is Forever. The only thing better than being with Christ is being with Christ forever. What a thought—heaven has no finishing point, no termination, no closeout date. It begins at the point of death and never comes to an end. Because the everlasting God Himself preserves it, heaven will exist in perfection for all of eternity (Revelation 22:5).

When my wife and I were engaged, we greatly looked forward to the time we would be married. We could hardly wait for the day we would promise ourselves to each other. Yet, even in our vows, we admitted that our marriage would not last forever. In fact, we knew it would last only "as long as we both shall live." Our marriage is temporary in that it is limited to this life.

While on this earth, our relationship to Christ is similar to the engagement period between a man and a woman. Christ has promised Himself to us, and we have promised ourselves to Him. We are His bride, the church; and we anticipate, with much eagerness, the day when we will be with Him. Yet, when we get to heaven and partake in the marriage supper of the Lamb (Revelation 19:7–9), our union with Christ will not be merely temporary. Rather, it truly will last forever. "Until death do us part" will not be necessary—death will no longer exist.

People are always curious about the future. "What will I be doing in five years, ten years, twenty years?" "Where will I be when my kids are in college?" "How old will I be when I retire?" Unfortunately, when considering the future, most Christians only think about their earthly lives—the seventy-five or eighty years we share on this planet. When was the last time you asked yourself, "What will I be doing a thousand years from now? Or, ten thousand?" According to God's Word, His children will be with Him in heaven—worshiping and serving Christ. When we start to think in light of eternity, this short life suddenly gets put in the proper perspective.

We can work hard here, because heaven is everlasting rest. We can suffer here, because heaven is everlasting peace and safety. We can survive trials here, because heaven is everlasting joy. Anything temporary can be endured or thrust aside because our focus is on what really matters, laying up treasures that will last forever.

5. You Can Hope in Heaven Because Heaven Is Not Hell. Although the focus of this chapter is on the glories of heaven, it is appropriate by contrast to briefly mention the horrors of hell. After all, we cannot fully appreciate the wonder of God's grace in offering us the hope of heaven unless we also consider the terrible alternative.

While not a popular doctrine, often dismissed as religious manipulation that is incompatible with God's love, Scripture is very clear—hell is just as real as heaven. In fact, to deny the existence of hell is to seriously question the existence of heaven, since the Bible is equally dogmatic about both.

The Bible says that hell lasts forever (Matthew 25:46; Revelation 20:10) as a place of punishment for those who have rejected God's offer of salvation (John 3:36; Revelation 14:9–11). Described as a place of physical torment (Isaiah 66:24) and mental anguish (Luke 16:23–28), hell is a place of total separation from God's love—it is the culmination of His wrath. In contrast to many contemporary cartoons, hell is not ruled by Satan and his minions. In fact, they are its chief captives (Matthew 25:41; Revelation 20:10–15). Joining them will be unsaved men and women who have rejected the sacrifice of Christ (John 5:28–29). Having rebelled against an eternal God, they must pay an eternal penalty.

While not our favorite place to think about, the reality of hell reminds Christians just how thankful they should be for their God-given hope. In contemplating eternal punishment, we are confronted with the magnitude of God's grace and Christ's sacrifice—without which heaven would be inaccessible.

THIS WORLD IS NOT OUR HOME

Thankfully, for those of us in Christ, the torments of hell will never be our experience. They should have been—because we are sinners. Yet, God offers us heaven through Christ Jesus, making us heirs of eternal life and citizens of the celestial city (Philippians 3:20–21).

In light of this, the church's constant preoccupation with worldly interests is confusing. Sometimes I hear passionate believers being accused of being so heavenly minded that they are no earthly good. Yet, I fear that many in our congregations are just the opposite—they are too earthly minded to be of any heavenly value. They have placed a higher priority on temporary comfort than on eternal reward. As a friend's father once told me, "Looking for heaven on earth is hell."

With this in mind, C. S. Lewis aptly notes, "I find in myself a desire which no experience in this world can satisfy, the most probable explanation is that I was made for another world."[4] Indeed, this earth is not our home. . .our home is in heaven. Maybe it's time we acted like it.

MEASURING SUCCESS
IN TERMS OF ETERNITY:
Hope Is a Perspective (Part 1)

His [God's] pleasure is not in the strength of the horse, nor his delight in the legs of a man;
the LORD delights in those who fear him, who put their hope in his unfailing love.

PSALM 147:10–11

I have been profoundly impressed with the sacrifices made by Christian men and women throughout the centuries of church history. From martyrs to missionaries, these individuals have served their King with greatest intensity and courage, valiantly standing as examples for those who come behind them. They are individuals of whom "the world was not worthy" (Hebrews 11:38) because their eyes were not set on the worth of this world, but rather on the values of heaven.

Adoniram Judson, as one of North America's first missionaries, was one of these individuals. Never to return, Judson and his wife, Nancy, left from Massachusetts in 1812. Their missionary endeavors, taking them first to India and later to Burma (present-day Myanmar), would prove to be wrought with suffering and tragedy.

They underwent economic challenges, losing the financial backing of their supporters only a few months after leaving the United States. Their plans unexpectedly changed when problems with their visas in India forced them to reluctantly settle in Burma. They faced a severe language barrier that required them to learn the Burmese tongue in a country where no English was spoken. Once they could communicate, their message still met with great resistance from the Burmese citizens. In fact, the Judsons did not see anyone come to Christ for the first six years of their work. And, by the end of Adoniram Judson's life, some of these so-called believers had openly denied Christ. The few who remained faithful were rewarded with intense government persecution. Judson, himself, was also in danger. Suspected of being a spy during Burma's civil war, he was sent to a death prison where he was hung upside down in leg irons every night and forced on a death march that almost killed him. In addition, Judson faced the pain of loss some two dozen times, burying both his first and second wife. In fact, from 1812 to 1850, twenty-four of Judson's relatives or close associates died, including several of his children. As a husband, father, missionary, and friend, Judson truly knew what it was to suffer. Nevertheless, enduring all of this, he steadfastly pursued his goal of translating the Bible into Burmese. In 1850 he died in obscurity, leaving a Burmese church with only a handful of believers.

By earthly standards, Judson's life was an utter failure. He jeopardized the lives of his family; he moved far away from the comforts of his North American roots; he endured the pain of rejection, hunger, torture, and loss; and he did all of this to bring the gospel to a generally unreceptive, antagonistic audience. He gave his all, only to die seeing relatively meager results.

In looking back, of course, we see that Judson's efforts were not in vain. In fact, his translation of the Bible is still used in Myanmar today. In 1993, the head of the Myanmar Evangelical Fellowship stated, "Today, there are 6 million Christians in Myanmar, and every one of us traces our spiritual heritage to one man—the Reverend Adoniram Judson."[1]

Yet, Judson never saw the great fruits of his labors. Nonetheless, he remained faithful because he hoped in a faithful God. He did not measure the success of his toil in terms of human expectations, but rather in terms of heaven's promise.

Clearly, Judson's outlook on life is far different than that of many Christians today. Because of his confident hope in the Lord's promises, he was able to see the eternal value of his work, even when the immediate results seemed miniscule; his Christ-centered focus allowed him to see things from God's point of view. As with all of us, Judson's values determined his viewpoint. In his case, those values clearly reveal the steadfast nature of his heaven-anchored hope.

Imagine if today's church shared this same perspective on life—a perspective driven by a hope-filled value system and unaffected by the momentary afflictions of this world. Believe it or not, this is the very perspective every Christian should have (2 Corinthians 4:17–18). Sadly, however, many of us have become nearsighted (2 Peter 1:9–10) and are badly overdue for a spiritual eye exam. We need to be reminded that our focus should be on God's promises and not on the temporary pursuits of this earth. With this in mind, we will spend the next three chapters investigating five viewpoints that hope changes—five areas in which hope radically alters the Christian's worldview.

1. Hope Changes the Way We View Life. The first perspective that hope impacts is the way we view life. Hope focuses our lives, giving us purpose and meaning—motivating us to keep on doing what God wants us to do and helping us align our every moment with realities of eternity. In other words, God's promises, when truly embraced, have a dramatic impact on both how we spend our time and how we use our resources.

a. *Hope keeps accurate time.* Our society is obsessed with the clock. We schedule every event carefully, keep multiple clocks in each room of our houses, and set our watches five minutes ahead just to be safe. If the bus is late, we grumble; if the wait is long, we never come back; and if the sermon goes over, we stop paying attention. Wasting time is anathema, at least in theory. It was Seneca who said, "We are always complaining that our days are few, and acting as though there would be no end."

God's Word agrees with the fact that life is short (Psalm 90:10–12). Yet, Scripture's view of time is diametrically opposed to that of many in the world. Instead of being wasted on temporal fulfillment (because once you die, life is over), the Bible teaches that time should be spent seeking God's kingdom (because once you die, true life begins).

Because death could come at any moment (Ecclesiastes 8:7, 9:12), Christians should make the most of every opportunity God gives them. Because Christ could come back at any time (1 Thessalonians 4:13–18), believers should eagerly await His arrival, being diligent during His absence so that He will be pleased with us at His return (Luke 19:12–27; Philippians 3:20). Because the pursuits of this world are passing away (1 Corinthians 7:31; 1 John 2:17), Christians should seek the everlasting treasures of heaven. After all, if our hope is in this world, our hope will die with us. But, if our hope is in God's eternal promises, it will never die. We can spend our lives sacrificing worldly comfort and indulgence because we know that one day we will have eternal rest and joy.

b. *Hope pursues what is truly valuable.* Hope views wealth the same way it views time—in light of the promises of God's Word. While the materialists of this world chase after the temporal, Jesus commands us to pursue what is spiritually valuable (Matthew 6:19–21).

King Solomon was a man who hoped to find satisfaction and value in the things of this world. Because of his great wisdom and wealth, he had both the intellectual and financial capability to dabble in everything his heart desired. As we will see in chapter 12, he experimented with pleasure, alcohol, wealth, amusement, romance, fame, accomplishment, and intelligence. Yet, at the end of all this, Solomon laments that all of it "was meaningless, a chasing after the wind; nothing was gained under the sun" (Ecclesiastes 2:11). In fact, it is not until the end of Ecclesiastes that Solomon underscores what life is truly about: "Here is the conclusion of the matter: Fear God and keep his commandments, for this is the whole duty of man" (Ecclesiastes 12:13).

Instead of hoping for happiness in the temporal and the vain, true hope values what God values, because it views life from His perspective. Hope seeks after those things that last forever, believing that God will reward the faithfulness of His children.

2. Hope Changes the Way We View Ourselves. Focusing on God's promises not only changes the way we view life, it also changes the way we view ourselves. Commonly called self-awareness, the view people have of themselves continues to become an increasingly popular topic. Walk into your average bookstore and you're bound to find a self-help section. Self-love, self-esteem, self-fulfillment—these are all terms expressing people's desperate attempts to get in touch with who they really are. Of course, the Bible also has a lot to say about how we view ourselves. And, again, the doctrine of hope plays a major role.

a. *Hope relies on its Savior, not itself.* In contrast to today's emphasis on self-reliance and self-preservation, hope mandates that we trust in the Lord rather than in ourselves. It is His sacrifice that saves us and not our own works (Romans 5:10). It is His righteousness that covers us, not our own good deeds (Romans 3:22). By hoping in God, we admit we cannot save ourselves. We must look to someone else, namely, Jesus Christ.

For this reason, the hope-filled life is one of humility. The arrogance of the self-sufficient leaves no room for a Savior. After all, salvation is a gift from God "not by works, so that no one can boast" (Ephesians 2:9). The promises of eternal life and heavenly reward should not make us boastful, but thankful. God didn't choose us because we were special. In fact, God delights in choosing the weak and the lowly so He can display His glory through our frailty (1 Corinthians 1:27–29; Jeremiah 9:23–24). As a result, all of the glory for our hope goes only to God.

b. *Hope pursues God's kingdom over personal comfort.* Not only does hope demand a sense of self-worthlessness, in that we cannot save ourselves; it also demands a life of selflessness, in that we must no longer live for ourselves. When discussing the cost of following Him, Jesus said, "If anyone would come after me, he must deny himself and take up his cross daily and follow me. For whoever wants to save his life will lose it, but whoever loses his life for me will save it" (Luke 9:23–24). And, in comparing salvation to a precious pearl, Christ implies that we must be willing to give up everything as His disciples (Matthew 13:46). In Mark 8:35–36, He reiterates this point: "Whoever wants to save his life will lose it, but whoever loses his life for me and for the gospel will save it. What good is it for a man to gain the whole world, yet forfeit his soul?"

While these verses do not teach that Christians must seek martyrdom or sell all of their belongings in order to be obedient, they do teach that believers must be *willing to do so*. Of course, the willingness to sacrifice everything for Christ is only possible when He truly is the Christian's hope. Do you want to know if Christ is truly the center of your hope? Ask yourself if you would be willing to give up your family to follow Him (Luke 14:26–27). What about your next meal (Philippians 4:12–13) or your home (Matthew 8:20)? Would you even be willing to give your life (Matthew 16:24)?

Until His kingdom is given first priority (Matthew 6:33), the would-be disciple will always struggle with putting too much stock in the false hopes of this world. It is only when we deny ourselves (and our worldly desires) that we can truly begin to value the things of heaven.

SEEING THINGS FROM GOD'S PERSPECTIVE

In the next two chapters, we will continue to look at how hope changes the way a Christian looks at life. While most see life as a onetime opportunity to pursue personal success and pleasure, the hope-filled Christian sees life as a staging ground for eternity. Personal comfort, achievement, and wealth are not important. What is important is serving the Savior who promises to reward those who are faithful (Revelation 22:12).

Adoniram Judson was this type of hope-filled Christian. He spent his life in toil and discomfort. He died in obscurity, relatively unknown. Yet, because of his eternal perspective, he was willing to deny himself and invest his life in the bank account of heaven. As a result, by God's grace, six million names have already been added to the Lamb's Book of Life. More and more join them every day. From an earthly standpoint, Judson was a failure. But from God's point of view, he was a total success. Like Adoniram Judson, Christians must fix their eyes on the hope of Christ's kingdom—denying themselves and living each day in service to Him.

CHAPTER 8

IN THE MIDST OF THE STORM:
Hope Is a Perspective (Part 2)

Why are you downcast, O my soul? Why so disturbed within me?
Put your hope in God, for I will yet praise him, my Savior and my God.

PSALM 42:11

It seems as though hardship follows some people through life more closely than others. Horatio Spafford was one of those people. A wealthy Chicago attorney, committed Christian, and close friend of D. L. Moody, his story has been told many times. Yet, like a nineteenth-century Job, his sufferings only heightened the tenacity of his faith, setting him apart as an example of the hope-filled life. In the midst of personal devastation, his proper perspective prevailed.

Spafford's trials began with the tragic loss of his only son who died of pneumonia at age four. Shortly thereafter the Great Chicago Fire of October 1871 nearly ruined him financially—when the waterfront properties in which he had heavily invested literally went up in smoke. In light of these hardships and in order to support his friend's ministry, Spafford decided to take his family on a European vacation (which included participating in a British evangelistic campaign with

Moody). The trip was scheduled for November 1873.

Spafford's plans, however, were interrupted. The day before his family's departure, he was notified that he must attend a mandatory meeting in Chicago regarding the removal of postfire wreckage. If he did not attend, he would risk losing his property holdings, so he reluctantly chose to temporarily delay his passage to Europe. Nonetheless, he sent his wife, Anna, and four daughters on ahead, planning to join them a short time later. Never did he imagine that his family's ship, the SS *Ville du Havre*, would never reach its intended destination. Striking another vessel while at sea, it sank to the ocean floor in less than fifteen minutes. All four of Spafford's daughters—Tanetta, Maggie, Annie, and Bessie—were killed. Incredibly, his wife survived, sending Spafford the tragic telegram: "Saved alone."

Having received the news, Spafford immediately left Chicago to rejoin his wife in Wales. En route, he came to the approximate place where his daughters had died. Spafford would later recount that, at that very moment, he felt peace like a river despite the billowing sorrows of the surrounding sea. Needless to say, it was Spafford's hope in God that allowed him to respond to his grief by writing the well-known hymn "It Is Well with My Soul." Despite the hardships of his life, he found comfort and consolation in the fact that his soul was in God's secure hands.

Put yourself in Spafford's shoes. Your only son has recently died. Your major investments have been burned to the ground. Your finances are depleted, your plans have been interrupted, and all four of your daughters have drowned in a bizarre boating accident. How would you respond? Would you be angry with God? Would you question His wisdom? Or would you embrace Him all the more, clinging that much more tightly to His promises?

3. Hope Changes Our Perspective on Suffering and Trials. Suffering is never easy, otherwise it wouldn't be suffering. Yet, the trials of life should never cause us to doubt God's plans or promises.

In fact, Scripture highlights the spiritual value that difficult times can bring. It is through the fires of hardship that God purifies our lives, making us more mature in the process. While the pain is certainly real, the promised spiritual benefit is nevertheless greater. Hope allows us to smile at the future, even when storm clouds loom on the horizon.

Personal trials come in all shapes and sizes. Sometimes it is something as simple as a leaky faucet or a malfunctioning alarm clock. Often, however, our troubles are considerably more serious— a death in the family, the discovery of a life-threatening illness, the threat of a terrorist attack, or the inability to pay next month's rent. Yet, no matter the situation or the supposed cause, Christians can trust in the fact that God is in control (2 Chronicles 29:8). He is our help and our refuge (Psalms 50:15, 59:16). And He will only allow us to experience that which is both possible for us to handle (1 Corinthians 10:13) and for our spiritual good (Romans 8:28).

With this in mind, we can rejoice even in the severest of seasons (James 1:2–4). From David (Psalm 42:11) and Daniel (Daniel 6:10) to Paul and Silas (Acts 16:25), Scripture shows that the proper response to trouble is not anxiety or anger, but rather thanksgiving (Philippians 2:14, 4:6). For those who are faithful, God has promised both future reward (2 Corinthians 4:16–17) and present spiritual growth. Andrew Murray summarizes it this way:

> First, He brought me here, it is by His will I am in this strait place: in that fact I will rest. Next, He will keep me here in His love, and give me grace to behave as His child. Then, He will make the trial a blessing, teaching me the lessons He intends me to learn, and working in me the grace He means to bestow. Last, in His good time He can bring me out again—how and when He knows. Let me say I am here, (1) By God's

appointment, (2) In His keeping, (3) Under His train-ing, (4) For His time.[1]

As we will see in chapter 13, God often brings trials into our lives in order to remind us to keep our focus on Him. It is often when the false hopes of this world have gained our attention that God allows hardship to invade our lives. This is not as a cruel joke or some type of angry retribution. It is His loving discipline (Hebrews 12:5–7), correcting our misplaced priorities and bringing our focus back into proper alignment. C. S. Lewis says this:

> *I am progressing along the path of life in my ordi-nary contented condition, when suddenly a stab of pain threatens serious disease, or a newspaper headline threatens us all with destruction.*
>
> *At first I am overwhelmed, and all my little happi-nesses look like broken toys. And perhaps, by God's grace, I succeed, and for a day or two become a creature con-sciously dependent on God and drawing its strength from the right sources. But the moment the threat is withdrawn, my whole nature leaps back to the toys.*
>
> *Thus the terrible necessity of tribulation is only too clear. God has had me for but 48 hours and then only by dint of taking everything else away from me. Let Him but sheathe the sword for a minute, and I behave like a puppy when the hated bath is over—I shake myself as dry as I can and race off to reacquire my comfortable dirtiness in the nearest flower bed.*
>
> *And that is why tribulation cannot cease until God sees us remade.*[2]

Certainly, trials are not the most pleasant times in life. Yet, by

God's grace, they always turn out for His glory and our spiritual benefit. For this reason, we can continue to place our hope in God and His promises.

4. Hope Changes the Way We View Sin. God is not the only One who makes promises to His children. In fact, there are many who promise satisfaction, joy, and fulfillment apart from God. For example, Satan, this worldly system, and even our fallen flesh—they all promise that happiness is found in sin rather than in obedience. Yet, their assurances always prove to be empty and false.

In the end, the question is: Which set of promises are you going to believe? On the one hand, you have the eternal guarantees of a faithful God who loves you and knows what is in your best interest. The Bible says that true hope is founded on these promises. When God says only He can give total satisfaction, we should believe Him—choosing to trust and obey. On the other hand, you face the constant bombardment of temptation, with the promises of sin telling you that happiness is actually found in disobedience. Obviously, someone is lying. After all, the two sets of promises cannot both be true.

When we sin, we are in essence saying that God is a liar. We have chosen to believe the promises of sin over the promises He gives us in His Word. But when our hope is firmly placed in God, temptation's alluring call loses its power, because we realize it is simply a mirage. God's promises are the only ones that are actually true.

The famous church father Augustine described sin this way:

> *Sin comes when we take a perfectly natural desire or longing or ambition and try desperately to fulfill it without God. Not only is it sin, it is a perverse distortion of the image of the Creator in us. All these good things, and all our security, are rightly found only and completely in him.*[3]

In fact, Christ was tempted in this way. Satan tempted Him with physical provision (Matthew 4:3–4), public recognition (Matthew 4:5–7), and political power (Matthew 4:8–10). Surely Jesus, as God in human flesh, deserved each of these things. Moreover, these things are not even bad in and of themselves. Yet, because they were not part of the Father's plan for Christ at that time, to fulfill those desires would have been sin on Jesus' part. Jesus, using God's Word as a defense with each temptation, chose to rest in God's perfect plan rather than trust in Satan's lies. As the Son of God, Jesus knew whose promises to believe—His Father's.

THE GOOD, THE BAD, AND THE UGLY

As we travel through this life, we find ourselves in a wide variety of different circumstances and situations. Many of these are good—wonderful times spent with family, friends, and fellow Christians. In these times it seems easy to keep our eyes on God and His promises. After all, life is good and the future is even better.

But life also has its bad and ugly moments. The bad times—trials and hardship—can come on both a personal and a public level. Sometimes the crisis is just within our closest circles, or maybe it is ours to bear alone. At other times, the problem is national or maybe even global. Feelings of anger, doubt, and fear can begin to build as anxiety becomes a way of life. God's Word, however, commands us to take our eyes off of the storm and put them back on Christ. He has promised to see us through. He is the anchor that holds us (Hebrews 6:19–20).

The ugly times—temptation and fleshly desires—also bombard the Christian life. Yet, the believer need not fear. God has given us the proper weapons to defend against the enemy's attack (Ephesians 6:10–18). Of course, we must trust His promises in these times, too.

He has promised not to let us encounter more than we are able to bear. He has promised that His Word is a more-than-adequate defense. He has promised that only He can satisfy (Proverbs 19:23; Jeremiah 2:13; Hebrews 13:5). And He has promised that obedience leads to blessing, while disobedience leads to devastation and self-destruction (Proverbs 19:16). Because we have been saved, we do not have to sin (Romans 8:1–4). It is in choosing to put our hope in the words of our Father, rather than the lies of the tempter, that we are guaranteed the victory.

In each of these areas—when life is good, bad, or ugly—God's promises should impact our lives dramatically, promoting thankfulness, trust, and purity. Consequently, if we keep our eyes on Christ, we can live faithfully and righteously, no matter what life brings our way.

CHAPTER 9

A HOPE WORTH DYING FOR:
Hope Is a Perspective (Part 3)

If we live, we live to the Lord; and if we die, we die to the Lord.
So, whether we live or die, we belong to the Lord.

ROMANS 14:8

Foxe's Book of Martyrs is a must read for every Christian. Written by John Foxe over 350 years ago, it catalogs the lives of hundreds of believers who, throughout church history, were willing to give their lives for the cause of Christ. When it comes to contagious courage, I can think of no greater testimony than reading about those who embraced their Lord to the point of embracing death.

One such account concerns the lives of Jerome Russell and Alexander Kennedy, two English Protestants who took a daring stand for what they believed. Because of their biblically sound doctrine, the pair was arrested and imprisoned. Kennedy was only eighteen years old. After some time, the two men were brought before religious officials for questioning. Russell, being older, gave an articulate defense, using the Scriptures to support his belief in salvation through faith alone. Yet, in spite of the evidence, the men's accusers prevailed and Russell and Kennedy were deemed heretics. In keeping with the jurisprudence of the times, they were condemned to death—their sentence to be carried out the following day.

Early the next morning, Russell and Kennedy were led from their prison cells to the place of execution. They could have denied their Lord, right then and there, and been spared. But when Kennedy, being but a young man, began to display signs of fear, Russell quickly encouraged him to stand firm:

> *Brother, fear not; greater is He that is in us, than he that is in the world. The pain that we are to suffer is short, and shall be light; but our joy and consolation shall never have an end. Let us, therefore, strive to enter into our Master and Savior's joy, by the same straight way which He hath taken before us. Death cannot hurt us, for it is already destroyed by Him, for whose sake we are now going to suffer.*

In this way, the two men came to boldly face execution without compromise. John Foxe finishes the account with this.

> *When they arrived at the fatal spot, they both kneeled down and prayed for some time; after which being fastened to the stake, and the fagots [kindling] lighted, they cheerfully resigned their souls into the hands of Him who gave them, in full hopes of an everlasting reward in the heavenly mansions.*

How could these men calmly submit to being burned alive? Why did they willingly undergo severe suffering and death? The answer here, again, begins with the doctrine of hope. By focusing on the promises of heaven and the faithfulness of God, they stood firm as a testimony to the truth. Clearly, hope had changed their perspective—even on something as grave as death.

5. Hope Changes the Way We View Death. Every day over five thousand people die. Some die from disease, others from crime, and still others from tragic accidents. Sometimes death is expected, the prognosis having been grim for several months; other times death is unforeseen and sudden—the result of an unexpected stroke or a drunk driver. But no matter how it comes, all of us know that one day it will be our turn. Death is part of life, and there's no escaping it.

One might think that, due to its widespread inevitability, death is something people would ponder frequently, constantly preparing for the end of their earthly lives. Yet, generally speaking, the opposite seems to be the case. People feel uncomfortable talking about death, usually preferring to avoid the subject. After all, death is the great unknown. It is the result of tragedy, the basis of fear, and the ultimate separation from friends and family.

Of course, it's understandable to realize that non-Christians cower at the thought of dying. For them it is the end of everything they hold dear. The pleasures of this earth, its resources and relationships—this is all they have. In dying, they lose what they have worked so hard to obtain.

What's sad is when those in the church embrace this same worldly perspective. Why should a Christian ever fear the grave? Is not death the doorway to heaven? Is there not eternal life on the other side? God's Word is clear: Death has been swallowed up in victory (1 Corinthians 15:56–57). Granted, when we hope in the pursuits of this world, death is the enemy—separating us from the temporal treasures we love. But, when our hope is properly placed in God, death comes as a welcome friend to take us home. Here are two reasons why:

a. *Hope sees death as a beginning, not an end.* The first reason that

Christians can embrace death is because, for believers, death is the beginning of a heavenly eternity. Death is not termination but initiation—the start of an existence far better than anything we can imagine. The apostle Paul knew this to be true. The book of 2 Timothy is the last letter he wrote before his execution—chapter 4 indicates that he realized his death was imminent (see v. 6). As he looked back on his life, he realized that his life was almost over (v. 7). Yet, he now looked forward to something far greater: namely, the reward of Jesus Christ and an eternity spent together with Him (v. 8). Paul looked beyond the grave and saw his God. Because Christ had conquered death (1 Corinthians 15:20–28) there was nothing to fear. It was John Owen, the great Puritan, who wrote on his deathbed: "I am yet in the land of the dying, but I hope soon to be in the land of the living." Like Paul, he too understood that true life, in its fullest measure, begins where this life ends.

In stark contrast, many in the contemporary church live as though this present life is better than the life to come. Tenaciously, they hold on to their short stay on this earth. Some follow every health fad, taking whatever supplement will reduce the risk of a heart attack. Others avoid airplanes, fearful that their trip could end in an unexpected dive. Our quest for longevity has affected our eating habits, our exercise routines, our travel plans, and even the type of sunscreen we buy. And while there is nothing inherently sinful in enjoying the earthly life that God has given, Christians sometimes need to be reminded that the next life is far superior. Death is a doorway, not a dead end. And for God's children, death's door opens into heaven.

b. *Hope sees the Shepherd through the shadows.* A second reason Christians need not fear death is because our Savior has already conquered death. He is not asking us to go anywhere He has not already been. And, because He arose from the grave victorious (Acts 2:32–33), we can be confident that we will also one day be resurrected (1 Corinthians 15:20).

In Psalm 23:4, the writer says, "Even though I walk through the valley of the shadow of death, I will fear no evil, for you are with me; your rod and your staff, they comfort me." For David, whose life was often in danger, comfort came in looking to his Shepherd, even when thinking about death.

Just over one thousand years later, an early Christian leader named Ignatius shared David's confident perspective. According to church tradition, Ignatius was arrested by the Roman government and executed because he professed Christ. Shortly before his death, he wrote the church of Rome, saying:

> *I care for nothing, of visible or invisible things, so that I may but win Christ. Let fire and the cross, let the companies of wild beasts, let breaking of bones and tearing of limbs, let the grinding of the whole body, and all the malice of the devil, come upon me; be it so, only may I win Christ Jesus.*

Even in being thrown to hungry animals and torn limb from limb, Ignatius's commitment to his Lord remained firm. He was willing to endure death because of the Master he sought to please, the Master he knew he would soon see face-to-face.

In considering death, these men focused on the One who was waiting to meet them there. They did not fear death because they rested in the promises of their Savior. What comes into your mind when you think about death? Maybe you think about the pain involved. Or maybe it's the cause of your death or the timing of it. Maybe you picture your funeral, wondering who is going to attend. Might I suggest, however, that a biblical perspective thinks first about Christ. And for the soul that loves Jesus, nothing is more exciting than the thought of going to be with Him. We love Him because He first loved us (1 John 4:19), and not even death can separate us from that love (Romans 8:38–39).

FINDING THE COURAGE TO FACE DEATH

Put simply, people are generally afraid of death. Practically speaking, this fear is a gift from God, because it prevents people from taking unnecessary and harmful risks. However, if given highest priority, it can become an unhelpful obsession and an obstacle. After all, the Lord commanded His disciples to be willing to die for His sake (Luke 9:23–26). When it comes down to it, believers must fear God more than they fear dying. But where does a Christian find the courage to face death?

Courage, broadly defined, is the quality or state of mind that enables a person to face danger or difficulty, including death, with bravery and boldness. Yet, for the believer this definition must be taken one step further. It is one thing to remain calm and act bravely when the outcome is unknown. The losing armies of many a battle included men who were courageous. It's just that their courage was unfounded—they stood for a losing cause. They were brave, but they were defeated. Yet, in Christ, we know we have already won the victory. We will not be defeated. The God who cannot lie has promised us eternal life (Titus 1:2). As Christians, courage is more than just the ability to face death calmly—it is the ability to face death confidently, standing firm because we know with certainty what the outcome will be.

Hebrews chapter 11 has often been referred to as the "Hall of Faith." In it, the writer details the lives of numerous men and women who lived lives of steadfast courage. Although they were merely ordinary people, God used them in extraordinary ways—because they would not compromise their faith, even if it meant death.

And premature death did come to many of these biblical heroes.

In fact, in verses 36–38, the writer comments about those who were tortured and killed for the cause of Christ.

> *Some faced jeers and flogging, while still others were chained and put in prison. They were stoned; they were sawed in two; they were put to death by the sword. They went about in sheepskins and goatskins, destitute, persecuted and mistreated—the world was not worthy of them. They wandered in deserts and mountains, and in caves and holes in the ground.*

In all of these trials, their courage sprung from the bedrock of a God-centered faith (see Hebrews 11:13–16). Their hope was in Him, because they knew He was faithful.

It's easy for us, several millennia later, to admire the bravery of these men and women of God. What's not easy, however, is to follow in their footsteps. The author of Hebrews did not list these examples so that we would applaud from the sidelines. Rather, he gave them as a motivation, that we might courageously endure the trials of this life as we pursue Christ (see Hebrews 12:1–3). Sadly, the reason many in today's church lack the courage to face death is because they lack the faith essential to such courage. Faith does not focus on the "seen" things of this world (Hebrews 11:1). Rather, it looks to the unseen promises of God—our hope—and lives life accordingly.

THE LONG ROAD HOME

When I was in high school, I used to walk to and from campus every day. Our family lived very close to the school, so it wasn't a far walk—maybe a mile. Because our house was located on the top of a hill, the way to school was totally downhill. The fire road I traveled each morning was easily navigated because gravity was on my side. The road home, however, was another story. In the heat of the afternoon, with a backpack full of books and each step kicking up dust, I made my way back up that hill—one foot in front of the other.

Despite the difficulty, I enjoyed the trip home a lot more than I enjoyed the trip to school. The reason is simple: I was going home—and I liked home a lot better than I liked class. Sure, the journey was hard, but the end result was more than worth the trip. In other words, when I saw that hill, I saw home.

Death is a little bit like that journey. It looms like a big, intimidating mountain on the back side of campus. The road is dusty and barren—at times even treacherous and steep. There are shadows of uncertainty and hidden curves in the path. Maybe it would be better to just stay on the familiar school grounds. After all, this life is the known, death is the unknown. But who really wants to stay in class after the final bell rings? Who wants to be there any longer than they absolutely must? Especially when the pleasures of home and the fellowship of family are just up the hill.

Christians have so much to look forward to in death—beginning with Christ Himself. And, not only is Jesus waiting on the other side, but He—as the Good Shepherd—promises to guide His sheep as they make the journey. Certainly, it's easy for us to get distracted—thinking that ultimate happiness can be found on this earth. The reality, however, is that true satisfaction is only found in Christ. Death can be embraced because it takes us to Him.

Surveying the
SPECIFICS

God's Promises for the Present and the Future

CHAPTER 10

GOD'S PROOF OF PURCHASE:

The Hope of Eternal Security

And you also were included in Christ when you heard the word of truth, the gospel of your salvation.
Having believed, you were marked in him with a seal, the promised Holy Spirit,
who is a deposit guaranteeing our inheritance until the redemption of those who are God's possession—
to the praise of his glory.

EPHESIANS 1:13–14

What is the best gift you've ever received? Maybe it was a new car on your sixteenth birthday. Maybe it was a beautiful piece of jewelry or maybe an unexpected visit from a long-lost friend. In my life, between each Christmas and birthday, I've been blessed with some really wonderful presents. When I was only three years old, I received a shiny, black, three-wheeled Hot Cycle. My parents have since told me that I was actually more enthralled with the brown belt my grandmother gave me that same year. Soon, however, my infatuation with the belt wore off. My Hot Cycle, on the other hand, was good for several years of pedal-powered fun.

On my eighth birthday, I was given an even more special present— a puppy. After incessantly begging my dad and mom to let me have a dog, they finally gave in. I still remember driving to the local animal shelter and choosing the perfect canine for me. The puppy I selected was a black-and-white terrier mix. I named her "Spott" (in my eight-year-old mind the second *T* distinguished her as female), and she was a wonderful pet for her eight years of life.

My eleventh birthday was also a memorable one—as I awoke to find five inches of fresh snow on the ground. Being from southern California, where it very seldom snows, the soft white blanket was a welcome novelty. Of course, it barely lasted through the entire day; but the fact that school was canceled made it all worth it. Not wanting to miss the opportunity, I even strapped on some skis and zigzagged down our street.

Yet, as wonderful as each of these presents were, they pale when compared to the greatest gift of all—namely, the gift of salvation and eternal life. The Bible is clear: Salvation is God's gift (Romans 6:23; Ephesians 2:8) to those who repent and believe (John 3:16; Romans 10:8–10). In fact, salvation is His promise to all who ask (John 6:37), meaning that we can have complete confidence in the hope of eternal life because God has given us His guarantee (Titus 1:2). What could be better than the promise of a glorious eternity spent with God? Nothing in this universe can even compare. Our hope is truly out of this world.

In spite of these biblical promises, many Christians struggle with doubt, wondering if God might possibly revoke His gift of salvation as a punishment for sinful behavior. In the deep recesses of their hearts, there are many who quietly wonder: "Maybe if I do something bad enough, God won't love me anymore" or "Maybe what I did was too big for even God to forgive." Certainly, these fears are understandable. After all, what a tragedy it would be to find the pearl of great price and then lose it (Matthew 13:45–46) or to gain entrance into the kingdom of heaven only to later be removed (Matthew 7:21). However, these fears are not only unwarranted, they are unbiblical. In this regard, God's Word is quick to put our troubled hearts at ease, making it clear that salvation, once gained, can never be lost. In fact, God says He will never let go of any who are His (John 10:28–29). This is His promise—a promise that offers every believer great hope for this life.

HOPE REALIZES THAT SALVATION IS A GIFT

In discussing the security of salvation, it is important to realize that salvation truly is a gift. Were it something we earned, it would not be a gift at all. It would be payment. God's Word, however, is clear— if we received what we had earned, we would all deserve eternal death. But, in His grace, God offers us salvation through His Son. Paul could not be more clear when, in Romans 4:4–5, he says: "Now when a man works, his wages are not credited to him as a gift, but as an obligation. However, to the man who does not work but trusts God who justifies the wicked, his faith is credited as righteousness." And again, in Romans 6:23: "For the wages of sin is death, but the gift of God is eternal life in Christ Jesus our Lord." And once more in Ephesians 2:8–9: "For it is by grace you have been saved, through faith—and this not from yourselves, it is the gift of God—not by works, so that no one can boast."

God's gift is available to all who repent and believe (Revelation 22:17). After all, Christ says that He will not turn away any who come to Him on His terms (John 6:37). Because we could not earn salvation for ourselves (Romans 3:23), God chose to give us, by means of Christ's death, what we could never otherwise obtain— eternal life. Since we did nothing to obtain it, there is nothing we can do to lose it, either. In Romans 8:38–39, Paul argues that "neither death nor life, neither angels nor demons, neither the present nor the future, nor any powers, neither height nor depth, nor anything else in all creation [including our own sin], will be able to separate us from the love of God that is in Christ Jesus our Lord." Clearly, our salvation is secure in God's hands.

HOPE UNDERSTANDS THAT GOD IS NO CHARLATAN

Not only do hope-filled Christians understand that salvation is an unearned gift, they also realize that the Giver of salvation is absolutely trustworthy (see chapters 3 and 4). For this reason, when God promises that salvation can never be lost, believers can rest assured that their eternity is secure. In Proverbs 26:18–19, Solomon remarks: "Like a madman shooting firebrands or deadly arrows is a man who deceives his neighbor and says, 'I was only joking!'" Surely God would not promise us eternal life only to later take it away with a casual "Fooled you!" Life is not a giant hidden-camera television show in which God, as the ultimate prankster, tricks people into thinking they can trust Him when they really shouldn't. Nor is God a cosmic cop, waiting until we store up just enough violations to have our heavenly driver's license revoked. In fact, the Bible presents the opposite picture, depicting God as a protector and refuge (John 17:11). Romans 8:30 indicates that all who are called in the present will be glorified in the future. Certainly, God will finish what He starts. And, because He never breaks a promise (1 Samuel 15:29), we can be sure that His children will never be disowned.

HOPE CLINGS TO GOD'S ETERNAL GUARANTEE

So far we've seen that salvation is an undeserved gift and that the Savior is a trustworthy Giver. But God doesn't stop there—He gives us an additional reason to rejoice in the security of our salvation. While modern vernacular might use terms like "lifetime guarantee," "certificate of authenticity," or "warranty," God uses the term "seal"—referring to the ministry of the Holy Spirit whereby He ensures the eternal well-being of God's children. In other words, to guarantee that believers cannot lose their salvation, God seals them with His Holy Spirit. The Spirit is His proof-of-purchase, meaning that those who have the Spirit are thereby designated as those who have been saved.

Along these lines, in 2 Corinthians 1:21–22, Paul writes: "Now it is God who makes both us and you stand firm in Christ. He anointed us, set his seal of ownership on us, and put his Spirit in our hearts as a deposit, guaranteeing what is to come." In other words, the Holy Spirit is the Christian's pledge for the future as He marks out those who are saved. Other passages, such as 2 Corinthians 5:5 and Ephesians 1:13–14 echo this promise. All of God's children have been given His Spirit (Romans 8:13–17). And all who have been given His Spirit have been sealed. It follows, then, that all of God's children are guaranteed that their inheritance will never be taken away from them. (See also 1 Peter 1:3–5.)

GOD'S SEAL AT WORK

With the biblical evidence in, the verdict is clear—once a person is saved, he or she can never lose that salvation. After all, salvation is an unearned gift from a trustworthy Giver backed by an eternal guarantee. If we've been marked with God's seal, we need not worry about the future.

The fact that heaven is guaranteed, however, does not allow us to live lives of continual sin and disobedience. Salvation is not a twisted form of heavenly fire insurance, opening the door for lawless behavior while removing the threat of eternal consequences. In

Romans 6:2, speaking of those who would abuse God's forgiveness, Paul responds with an emphatic "By no means!" In contrast, Scripture teaches that God's children will not even want to live in patterns of unbroken sin—they do not want to disobey their Father.

In ancient times, a seal not only served as a guarantee, but also as a mark of ownership. By putting His seal on us, God has left His indelible impression on our lives through His Spirit. He has claimed us for Himself. In contemporary terms, we are under new management—namely, God's. While we once were slaves to the lusts of our flesh, we are now under the law of the Spirit (Romans 8:1–2; 9). This means that God is our Master and we are to submit to Him (John 14:15; Ephesians 6:9), pursuing holiness rather than sin (1 Peter 1:16). Those who live in long patterns of continued disobedience simply evidence the fact that God is not, and never has been, their owner (1 John 1:6). After all, God always disciplines those who are His, bringing them back to repentance (Hebrews 12:4–11).

In order to help us obey, God has given us the Holy Spirit as our helper and guide (John 14:16–17). In fact, He has given His Spirit to every person whom He has saved (1 Corinthians 12:13). And since being Spirit filled necessarily results in spiritual fruit (Galatians 5:22–23; Ephesians 5:18–20), those whom God has saved will evidence patterns of righteousness in their lives. His indelible seal will be recognizable, as an unmistakable mark, in the works that they do. After all, Jesus Himself taught that you can recognize the spiritual condition of others by the lives they lead (Matthew 7:15–21; Luke 6:43–44).

Of course, sanctification, or holy living, has always been God's plan for those whom He saves. In 2 Timothy 1:9, Paul indicates that when God saved us He "called us to a holy life." And 2 Thessalonians 2:13 says that from the beginning God designed salvation to involve "the sanctifying work of the Spirit." Of course, Ephesians 2:8–9 emphasizes that salvation is by grace apart from works. Yet, in verse 10, the writer continues by adding that one of God's intended purposes in saving us is that we might "do good works."

Clearly, salvation is a free gift that can never be lost. Nevertheless, it is not an excuse for loose living or self-indulgence. After all, God cleanses the hearts of His children (Titus 3:5–7) and clean hearts lead to pure lifestyles. Those whose lives do not reflect that kind of change of heart need to ask themselves some serious questions (2 Corinthians 13:5). Yet, for those whose lives reflect God's commands, the Spirit gives great assurance regarding the security of their salvation (Romans 8:16).

SAFE IN THE HAND OF GOD

What joy there is in knowing that Christians can never lose their salvation. We don't have to spend our lives worrying about whether God still loves us. We don't have to go to bed each night frightened that we might wake up on the wrong side of heaven. Our Savior has promised that He will accept all who come to Him in sincere repentance (John 6:37). He has promised that those who are saved will never be lost. They are safe in the hand of God, held securely for all eternity (John 10:28–29).

As a result, Christians can concentrate on living in light of our heavenly homeland, rather than constantly worrying if we have one. Eternal security is just another part of the believer's hope chest—one of the promises God has given to His children for both this life and the next. Isn't it comforting to know that in giving us an inheritance, God won't suddenly take it away? He gave us a gift and He's not going to take it back. Now there's a promise we can build our lives on.

CHAPTER 11

BECAUSE HE CARES FOR YOU:
The Hope of God's Daily Care

Do any of the worthless idols of the nations bring rain?
Do the skies themselves send down showers?
No, it is you, O LORD our God.
Therefore our hope is in you, for you are the one who does all this.

JEREMIAH 14:22

George Mueller was born in 1805 in modern-day Germany. As an unsaved young man, Mueller lived a life of sin even while training for ministry in the state church. His life changed dramatically, however, after he was converted at a small prayer meeting in a private home. Desiring to serve the Lord overseas, Mueller moved to England— seeking to work with the London Missionary Society. When his application was rejected, he decided to remain in England (in the town of Bristol), where he ministered for over thirty years.

In 1835, Mueller opened his first orphanage. Eventually, he would open four more, yet with each one he solicited no financial assistance or help. In fact, he refused to advertise the needs of the orphanages, choosing instead to rely only on prayer and his faith in

God. And God always provided. In fact, by 1870, his orphanages were daily housing and feeding some twenty-one hundred girls and boys, with every provision directly pointing to the hand of God.

Arthur T. Pierson wrote the first authorized biography of Mueller's life in 1899. In it, Pierson recounts numerous times when the orphanages were terribly short on either money or food. Yet, Mueller's faith remained undeterred. Instead of growing anxious or surrendering to doubt, he responded to his circumstances by getting on his knees to pray.

On one occasion the orphanage had only enough money to supply the children with one last evening meal. Because of their financial situation, there was no money left for breakfast the following morning. Mueller went home that night, and when no money came in, he went to bed, trusting that God would provide. Early the next morning, while praying, he went for a walk along a route he didn't usually take. After a short distance a friend met him and asked him to accept some money for the orphans. Mueller thanked the man and joyfully returned to the orphanage. God had answered his prayer by directing his morning walk along an unusual path.

Stories like this could easily be multiplied. Money was donated at exactly the right moment, delivery trucks broke down just up the street, and prayer requests were answered in ways that could only be explained by pointing to God's providence. Sometimes, the provision came in unexpected ways and at unexpected times, yet it always came. As a result, Mueller's life was one characterized by hope for the present. He believed in God's promise to supply everything he needed, and he clung to that promise each day of his life.

OUR NATURAL RESPONSE TO IMMEDIATE NEEDS

Sadly, when needs arise, the initial response of most people in the church today is not the response of George Mueller. Instead of responding with prayer and faith, we respond with fear and concern. Our minds race frantically with what might happen if we fail to find the needed resources. Maybe we utter a quick prayer for help, but ultimately we choose to rely on ourselves rather than on the Lord. Instead of finding peace in His promises, we lean on our own strength—a decision that naturally leads to worry.

Appropriately, the word *worry* comes from its Old English ancestor *wygran* which means "to strangle." In Middle English, *wygran* evolved into *worien*—a term that added the idea of killing by biting the throat, such that the victim was suffocated to death. *Worien*, for example, would have described the way a wolf attacks a lamb. By the sixteenth century, *worry* had come to refer to rough treatment and harassment, even including the idea of verbal assault. This naturally led to its seventeenth-century usage in which its primary meaning was "to bother, persecute, or distress." From here, *worry* moved to include not only the perpetrator but also the victim. The result is our modern meaning of either causing or being caused to feel distressed or troubled.[1]

The reason I find this particular etymology so fascinating is because I think its ancestry accurately describes what it does: Worry is emotional strangulation. It suffocates us, like a heavy weight upon our minds. When we're worried, we can't focus clearly or relax; we become irritable and fidgety; we can't think of anything else. We are like a lamb in the jaws of a wolf, swept away by the fearful possibilities of an unknown future. Our problems loom like clouds on the horizon, and we can see nothing but the storm. As Chuck Swindoll aptly notes, "Worry pulls tomorrow's cloud over today's sunshine."[2] Walter Kelly sums it up like this:

> *Worry is faith in the negative, trust in the unpleasant, assurance of disaster and belief in defeat. . . . Worry is wasting today's time to clutter up tomorrow's*

opportunities with yesterday's troubles. A dense fog that covers a seven-city-block area one hundred feet deep is composed of less than one glass of water divided into sixty thousand million drops. Not much is there but it can cripple an entire city. When I don't have anything to worry about, I begin to worry about that.[3]

YOU CAN HOPE IN GOD FOR YOUR IMMEDIATE NEEDS

Clearly, worry is disastrous. But instead of becoming anxious over life's daily necessities, God asks us to trust Him and His paternal care. Like a loving father, He promises to care for the immediate needs of His children. After all, if we can trust Him for our eternal salvation, we can certainly look to Him for our day-to-day provisions.

The people of Jesus' day were no different than people today—meaning that their knee-jerk response to problems was usually worry rather than faith. For them, anxiety came in the form of Roman soldiers, tax collectors, widespread disease, and potential crop failures. Yet, while sympathizing with their circumstances, Jesus never excused their anxiety. Instead, He commanded them to look in faith to their heavenly Father, rather than looking in anxious doubt at the hardships around them. In Matthew 6:25–33 Jesus says the following:

> *"Therefore I tell you, do not worry about your life, what you will eat or drink; or about your body, what you will wear... Who of you by worrying can add a single hour to his life? And why do you worry about clothes?...So do not worry, saying, 'What shall we eat?' or 'What shall we drink?' or 'What shall we wear?' For*

the pagans run after all these things, and your heavenly
Father knows that you need them. But seek first his
kingdom and his righteousness, and all these things will
be given to you as well."

Clearly, worry—even for the things of this life—should not be an option for the Christian. If we focus on the work of God's kingdom, He will take care of us. But what things has God promised to provide for us here and now? What can we expect to receive from Him as we trust Him daily? Jesus, just a few verses earlier, gives three answers to that question.

1. You Can Hope in God for Your Physical Provision. In Matthew 6:9–13, Jesus instructs His disciples how to pray. In so doing, He teaches us what the right things are to bring to God in prayer. The requests that Jesus outlines, specifically in verses 11–13, are the requests we should pray for, as well. Because Jesus tells us to pray for these things, and because they are promised elsewhere in Scripture, we can be sure that God will answer our prayer according to His timing and His plan.

The first of these requests is this: "Give us today our daily bread" (v. 11). This means we are to trust God for our physical provision on a day-to-day basis. We are not to be anxious about what the next day, week, or month will bring. Instead, we can trust Him for something as basic and as essential as bread—which represents all of the things people need to sustain physical life. There is absolutely no reason to worry because the omnipotent God of the universe is our Father. He will take care of those who are His.

Of course, this does not excuse laziness, a lack of diligence, or poor planning on our part. Even our ability to work and earn a living is a gift from God (compare Deuteronomy 8:18; 1 Corinthians 4:7; and James 1:17). Our response to our needs, then, should be both diligence and thankful trust—realizing that everything we have comes from above.

2. You Can Hope in God for Your Spiritual Pardon. The second request Christ instructs us to make is this: "Forgive us our debts, as we also have forgiven our debtors" (Matthew 6:12). In following the request for physical provision with the request for spiritual pardon, the Lord reminds His audience that life is much more than simply physical needs—we all have spiritual needs, too, the most basic of which is forgiveness.

Such forgiveness entails the removal of our sins from as far as the east is from the west (Psalm 103:12). We used to owe God an unpayable amount as we daily added to our list of sins, causing our debt to grow greater and greater. Yet God, because of the sacrifice of His Son on the cross, has given us complete forgiveness from the sins we commit each day. And, as we saw in the previous chapter, His forgiveness once granted will never be taken away.

Certainly our familial relationship with God is hampered through our sins (Psalm 66:18), yet when we confess and repent of these trespasses, He is quick to restore that relationship with us. And, as this verse indicates, we demonstrate God's forgiveness in our lives by willingly forgiving others (Ephesians 4:32–5:1).

3. You Can Hope in God for Your Spiritual Protection. Christ's third petition is this: "And lead us not into temptation, but deliver us from the evil one" (Matthew 6:13). We can trust that God will never lead us into any situation that is too great for us to handle through His power. Although the translation "temptation" is commonly employed here, Christ is probably referring more to trials than actual enticement to sin. After all, God does not tempt anyone to sin (James 1:13). So, the prayer here is that God would protect His children from succumbing to sin in the trials and tribulations they face. Along these same lines, Paul states in 1 Corinthians 10:13:

No temptation has seized you except what is common to man. And God is faithful; he will not let you be tempted beyond what you can bear. But when you are tempted, he will also provide a way out so that you can stand up under it.

The apostle Peter, also, in 2 Peter 2:9 assures his readers that "the Lord knows how to rescue godly men from trials."

Whether trials will come is not the issue. Part of living in a sin-stained world means enduring times of tribulation and hardship. Nevertheless, when those difficulties come, God promises to be our shelter during the storm (Psalm 61:4). God also promises to preserve His children spiritually at all times, meaning that when sin comes knocking at our door, God gives us the power to overcome any temptation. It is His Spirit that frees us from sin's power (Romans 8:2) and His armor that protects us from its snares (Ephesians 6:10–20). Clearly, He has equipped us with His resources—the question is whether or not we're going to use them.

TAKING EACH DAY BY FAITH

God has promised to take care of us, even in this life, on a daily level. These promises include both His physical provision, in that He cares for our daily needs, and His spiritual provision, in that He forgives our sin and gives us everything we need to fight temptation.

Why is it, then, that we find ourselves so often worrying about the day-to-day details of our lives? Do we not have a heavenly Father who loves us and cares for us? Why do we anxiously try to solve our problems by ourselves rather than running to Him? After all, Jesus taught us to pray in such a way that seeks God's provision. Our Father has promised to take care of us—our response should be diligent obedience and patient trust.

George Mueller understood that God's promises could be taken at face value—they were trustworthy, both for this life and the next. Our prayer lives would change dramatically if we shared Mueller's resolve. Our confidence in the face of adversity would increase, along with our willingness to take risks for the sake of the gospel. Our faith would grow, being hinged on the absolute guarantees of God and His Word. Indeed, it would be wonderful if, at the end of our lives, what was said of George Mueller could be said of us.

> *Nothing is more noticeable, in the entire career of this man of God, reaching through sixty-five years, than the steadiness of his faith and the steadfastness it gave to his whole character. . . . If Mr. Mueller had any great mission, it was. . .to teach men that it is safe to trust God's word, to rest implicitly upon whatever He hath said, and obey explicitly whatever He has bidden; that prayer offered in faith trusting His promise and the intercession of His dear Son, is never offered in vain; and that the life lived by faith is a walk with God, just outside the very gates [of] heaven.*[4]

CHAPTER 12

SATISFACTION GUARANTEED:

The Hope of Finding Complete Satisfaction in God

Command those who are rich in this present world not to be arrogant nor to put their hope in wealth,

which is so uncertain,

but to put their hope in God, who richly provides us with everything for our enjoyment.

1 TIMOTHY 6:17

Benjamin Franklin once said, "Content makes poor men rich; discontent makes rich men poor." Ironically, as one of America's founding fathers, Franklin described the paradox many in our nation face today. Although the United States is arguably the wealthiest nation in the world, Americans never seem to have enough; the richer we get, the poorer we become. In fact, a 1992 *U.S. News and World Report* showed that those who made under twenty-five thousand dollars each year believed they needed to make fifty-four thousand dollars in order to achieve the American Dream. And those who made one hundred thousand dollars thought they needed an average of $192,000. No matter how much people earned, they always thought they needed more.[1]

Simply put, we live in a society that never has enough. While we are always searching for satisfaction, we never seem to find it. "I Can't Get No Satisfaction" is more than just a popular song of yesteryear, it's a slogan and a summary. Commercials, advertisements, and billboards—they all promise that their products will satisfy, and yet we always need to buy more. The following story illustrates the folly of our widespread discontentment.

> [There was a] rich industrialist who was disturbed to find a fisherman sitting lazily beside his boat. "Why aren't you out there fishing?" he asked.
>
> "Because I've caught enough fish for today," said the fisherman.
>
> "Why don't you catch more fish than you need?" the rich man asked.
>
> "What would I do with them?"
>
> "You could earn more money," came the impatient reply, "and buy a better boat so you could go deeper and catch more fish. You could purchase nylon nets, catch even more fish, and make more money. Soon you'd have a fleet of boats and be rich like me."
>
> The fisherman asked, "Then what would I do?"
>
> "You could sit down and enjoy life," said the industrialist.
>
> "What do you think I'm doing now?" the fisherman replied as he looked placidly out to sea.[2]

Of course, discontentment and dissatisfaction are not exclusive to modern Western civilization. People throughout all ages have searched to find meaning, fulfillment, and happiness in their lives. Yet, sadly, they usually look in all the wrong places. In the end, it's not until they look to God that they find true satisfaction. In this chapter, we will contrast the lives of two men—one who was satisfied in God and one who learned the hard way. By looking at their lives, we will see that God promises satisfaction to those who fully hope in Him.

A Tale of Two Princes

Imagine with me that you have been born into a royal family. As part of that family, you can have anything your heart desires. You have worldwide fame and recognition, with everyone in your kingdom honoring you as their governing superior. You have unlimited riches and wealth, enabling you to purchase anything you could ever want. You have ultimate power and control because, with the exception of your father the king, there is no greater authority in all the land. In other words, you have endless resources at your disposal.

If this were your situation, what would you do with your wealth? How would you spend your time? How would you spend your money? What would you do with your power and influence?

What for us is only an imaginary scenario was actually the very situation for two of Scripture's most renowned characters: Moses and Solomon. Both grew up in royal families. Both had access to the best things that life could provide. Yet, each responded very differently—specifically in regard to their search for satisfaction.

The Paradigm of the Prince of Egypt

Although the son of Jewish slaves, Moses was adopted by Pharaoh's daughter and raised in the Egyptian royal court. In fact, he lived as a prince in Egypt until he was forty years of age. As a young boy, he ate at Pharaoh's table, received a royal education, and became familiar with royal customs. Josephus even states that, as a young man, Moses was a general in Pharaoh's army—repelling a significant

Ethiopian attack against Egyptian interests in the south.

From a worldly perspective, Moses had it all going for him. Yet, instead of putting his hope in the things of this earth, he rejected his royal past in favor of the promises of God. In fact, Hebrews 11:24–26 says this about Moses:

> By faith Moses, when he had grown up, refused to be known as the son of Pharaoh's daughter. He chose to be mistreated along with the people of God rather than to enjoy the pleasures of sin for a short time. He regarded disgrace for the sake of Christ as of greater value than the treasures of Egypt, because he was looking ahead to his reward.

You see, Moses realized that he couldn't find satisfaction in the riches of Egypt. He couldn't find ultimate fulfillment in earthly power or fame. Those things fade away. But the promise of an eternal reward—that is something that lasts forever. By looking to his Lord, rather than his own kingdom, Moses chose to find his contentment in God rather than worldly things.

Presumably long after Moses left Egypt, he penned the words to Psalm 90. In the first verse, he refers to the Lord as his "dwelling place." Verse 14 is especially telling—Moses says to God, "Satisfy us in the morning with your unfailing love, that we may sing for joy and be glad all our days." He understood that true satisfaction started with God—not with the possessions or positions of this earth. In light of this, Moses serves as a model that all of us should follow.

THE PARADOX OF THE WISEST MAN

In contrast, there is another prince mentioned in Scripture who responded to his position in life very differently—namely, Solomon. Of course, Solomon did not simply stay a prince; after his father King David died, he became king of Israel. In fact, his kingdom was the wealthiest and most influential of any in Israel's history. Israel's military and diplomatic strength was unsurpassed—meaning that for Israel, Solomon's reign was a time of prosperity and growth.

Shortly after his coronation, Solomon was visited by God in a dream (1 Kings 3:5–14). In that dream, God promised to give Solomon greater wisdom than any other king Israel had ever known. Even to this day, Solomon is best remembered for his legendary insight and understanding.

Ironically, however, despite his mental acumen, Solomon chose to look to the things of this world for satisfaction. In so doing, he failed to heed his own advice. In the book of Proverbs, which Solomon probably wrote early in his reign, he states: "The fear of the LORD leads to life: Then one rests content, untouched by trouble" (Proverbs 19:23). In other words, Solomon knew from the outset that contentment comes from the Lord and not from anything else.

Despite knowing all this, Solomon proceeded to experiment with life's pleasures—seeing if maybe he could find fulfillment in something on this earth. In fact, in Ecclesiastes 2, written at the end of his life, Solomon catalogs his disastrous attempts at earth-centered satisfaction.

1. Solomon hoped for satisfaction in pleasure (Ecclesiastes 2:1–3, 8). Solomon began his attempts at satisfaction with the simple pursuit of pleasure (v. 1)—a pursuit that basically entailed looking for lasting happiness by having a good time. Sometimes this came in the form of entertainment (the singers of verse 8), sometimes in the form of alcoholic intoxication (the wine of verse 3), and sometimes in the form of romantic fulfillment (the concubines of verse 8; see also 1 Kings 11:1–3). More or less, it came in any form the wisest man who ever lived could imagine. Yet, at the end of it all, he concluded, "But that also proved to be meaningless. 'Laughter,' I said, 'is foolish. And what does pleasure accomplish?' " (v. 2).

2. Solomon hoped for satisfaction in productivity (Ecclesiastes 2:4–6). Realizing that true happiness was not found in the party scene, Solomon turned to work. In so doing, he was quite successful. Listen to all the things he accomplished: "I undertook great projects: I built houses for myself and planted vineyards. I made gardens and parks and planted all kinds of fruit trees in them. I made reservoirs to water groves of flourishing trees." Yet, Solomon's creative pursuits, as impressive as they were, did not bring him lasting happiness (see v. 11). And because he came to realize that work was not the key to satisfaction, he continued searching for the answer.

3. Solomon hoped for satisfaction in possessions (Ecclesiastes 2:7–8). Solomon's next experiment involved his material possessions. He was so successful in this endeavor that, according to 2 Chronicles 9:22, "King Solomon was greater in riches and wisdom than all the other kings of the earth." With this in mind, it's almost an understatement when Solomon himself writes, "I bought male and female slaves and had other slaves who were born in my house. I also owned more herds and flocks than anyone in Jerusalem before me. I amassed silver and gold for myself, and the treasure of kings and provinces." Put simply, King Solomon was rich. He had everything money could buy. Yet, in spite of all his stuff, he was still not truly happy.

4. Solomon hoped for satisfaction in prominence (Ecclesiastes 2:9–10). When materialism failed, Solomon looked to his own glory and greatness for satisfaction. After all, he had a lot to boast in. He was wiser than anyone else and wealthier than anyone else. He had expanded Israel's borders and even built the temple. Yet, at the end of his life, Solomon looked back and admitted that all his accomplishments, activities to which he had looked for ultimate happiness, were meaningless. They could not satisfy. Solomon put it this way, "Yet when I surveyed all that my hands had done and what I had toiled to achieve, everything was meaningless, a chasing after the wind; nothing was gained under the sun" (v. 11).

5. Solomon hoped for satisfaction in mental prowess (Ecclesiastes 2:12–14). In a last-ditch effort to find satisfaction, Solomon looked to his own human intellect—the very wisdom that God had given him. When all else failed, maybe the academic pursuits of his incredible mind would make him happy (see verses 12–14). Yet, just like all of his other pursuits, Solomon ended up realizing that not even intellectualism can offer lasting satisfaction. In verse 17, he made this conclusion: "All of it is meaningless, a chasing after the wind."

6. Solomon ultimately realized that only God satisfies (Ecclesiastes 12:13–14). Throughout the rest of the book of Ecclesiastes, Solomon rehearses the same theme—nothing on this earth can bring lasting satisfaction. But, at the very end of the book, Solomon gives his reader hope. While admitting that there is nothing on earth that can truly satisfy—and Solomon tried it all—there is Someone in heaven who can. In Ecclesiastes 12:13, Solomon ends his book with these words, "Now all has been heard; here is the conclusion of the matter: Fear God and keep his commandments, for this is the whole duty of man." Simply said, ultimate fulfillment comes in fearing God, not in anything else.

YOU CAN HOPE IN BEING SATISFIED

The rest of Scripture agrees with Solomon's conclusion—that only God can offer lasting satisfaction. Moses understood this to be true. King David compared worshiping God with being satisfied by the finest of foods (Psalm 63:4–5). The Lord Jesus commanded His followers to find their treasure in heaven rather than on earth (Matthew 6:19–21). The apostle Paul looked to God for his contentment rather than to the things of this world; sometimes he had much, other times he had nothing, but in everything he found his joy in Christ and not his circumstances (Philippians 4:11–20; 1 Timothy 6:6–8). Even the writer of Hebrews, speaking to a group of persecuted Jewish Christians, urged them to find their satisfaction in their ever present Savior. In Hebrews 13:5, he writes, "Keep your lives free from the love of money and be content with what you have, because God has said, 'Never will I leave you; never will I forsake you.'"

Needless to say, God has promised that we can find our satisfaction, fulfillment, contentment, and joy in Him. We may look for it in other places, but like the wise Solomon, we will find out just how foolish worldly pursuits can be. As Christians, we should follow the example of Moses, who gave up the passing pleasures of sin in order that he might find lasting satisfaction in God.

Chapter 13

Life's Silver Lining:
The Hope of God's Grace in the Midst of Trials

*We rejoice in the hope of the glory of God. Not only so,
but we also rejoice in our sufferings, because we know that suffering produces perseverance;
perseverance, character; and character, hope.
And hope does not disappoint us,
because God has poured out his love into our hearts by the Holy Spirit, whom he has given us.*

ROMANS 5:2–5

Nobody likes hard times. Even the Bible recognizes that no trial "seems pleasant at the time, but painful" (Hebrews 12:11). Yet, as we saw briefly in chapter 8, God's Word tells us that we can still have joy in the midst of difficult circumstances (James 1:2–3). Of course, the joy isn't found in the situation itself, but rather in the outcome—knowing that God is growing us spiritually by forcing us to trust Him. Paul had the right perspective when he noted that "our light and momentary troubles are achieving for us an eternal glory that far outweighs them all" (2 Corinthians 4:17).

It's amazing how quickly the storms of life cause us to run to God. When life is good, it's easy to get sidetracked with the pleasures of this world—finding our security here rather than in heaven. But, when trials come, we realize that the things of this earth are only as solid as loosely packed sand. In our distress, we remember that God alone is our Rock, our Strength, and our Deliverer (Psalm 31:2–4). Trials, then, are really a blessing—because they bring us back to what really matters, namely, God Himself.

John Calvin (1509–1564) was a man who understood the benefit of trials because he realized that they pointed his eyes toward heaven. Although Calvin was a man of great reputation and influence, his focus was on gaining heavenly treasure rather than earthly riches. John Foxe says this about his life:

> *That a man who had acquired so great a reputation and such an authority, should have had but a salary of one hundred crowns, and refuse to accept more; and after living fifty-five years with the utmost frugality should leave but three hundred crowns to his heirs, including the value of his library, which sold very dear, is something so heroic, that one must have lost all feeling not to admire.*

In his *Institutes of the Christian Religion*, Calvin discusses the benefits that trials can bring. Because he so eloquently underscores the right viewpoint on trials, let's sit briefly at the feet of this sixteenth-century saint and listen to his perspective.[1] He points out four ways that hope points to the rainbow in the storm clouds, clinging to God's promise even during the hardest of times.

A MESSAGE OF HOPE FROM JOHN CALVIN

1. You Can Have Hope in Trials Because Trials Point Us Back to God.

No matter what kind of trouble afflicts us, we should always remember that it is not without a purpose. Rather, it comes in order that we might train ourselves to despise this present life and instead be encouraged to look forward to our heavenly future. For God certainly knows how tenaciously we cling to this life, because of our slavish love of this world. And so, in order to prevent us from clinging to it too strongly, He sends trials and tribulation into our lives, according to His wisdom, in order to remind us of the reality of eternity.

In short, our entire soul, ensnared by the allurements of the flesh, seeks its happiness on this earth. And so, in order to counter this disease, our Lord brings us back to our senses by introducing hardship into our lives. In other words, to prevent Christians from getting too comfortable with the temporary pleasures and peace of this life, God allows them to experience difficulty and pain. God's purpose in doing this to us is not for our harm, but rather that we might keep our eyes on Him.

Think about it, God may not want you to be rich, lest you trust in your riches rather than Him. God may not want you to be healed, lest you trust in your health rather than Him. God may not want you to be popular, lest you trust in your friends rather than Him. God may not want you to be married, lest you find your joy in marriage before you find your joy in Him. If God were to simply let us indulge in our worldly pursuits, we would quickly fall into vanity and pride—being puffed up with unwarranted confidence. Yet, in His grace, He lets us suffer, that we might stay focused on what really matters: namely, Him.

In this way, then, we profit greatly from the discipline of the cross—meaning that in suffering we learn that this life, by itself, is full of troubles, sorrow, and uncertainty. There is nothing here that can make us truly happy. The only thing we can hope for on this earth is constant struggle—a struggle that forces us to raise our eyes to heaven, in the hope of our eternal crown and reward. After all, our minds will never seriously desire the future until they have learned to despise the present.

2. You Can Have Hope in Trials Because Trials Keep Us from Clinging to This World. Christians often desperately try to serve two masters: God, on the one hand, and worldly possessions on the other. But, as Christ said in Matthew 6, this type of dualism is impossible to maintain. There is no middle ground between the two: The earth must either be worthless in our estimation, or it will keep us enslaved through our selfish desires. So, if we have any regard for eternity, we must work carefully to free ourselves from the chains of this world.

Granted, our lives are full of temptations and enticements to sin. The false hopes of this world claim the ability to give us ultimate delight, pleasure, and sweetness—yet, the temporary satisfaction of sin never lasts; the empty promises of sin are never what they seem. Then, when we find ourselves indulging in the futility of our flesh, the Lord sends affliction to remind us of what really matters; the Lord disciplines His children so that they might remember to find their satisfaction in Him.

How quickly we forget that our lives are nothing more than smoke or shadow. It's not until we see a funeral or visit a cemetery that the image of death is again pressed into our minds. And, at these times, we are quick to philosophize about the vanity of life and the hope of heaven. Even then, our best thoughts are only momentary. Our contemplation of eternity fades quickly and without a trace, passing away like the applause of an amused crowd before a fleeting spectacle.

It is as though, in acknowledging death with occasional words, we live in denial of our own mortality. Accordingly, God in His love reminds us of our frailty and weakness—by shaking up our circumstances. In so doing, He prompts us to remember the miserable condition of our earthly life, focusing our hearts instead on the glorious eternity that awaits.

3. You Can Have Hope in Trials Because Trials are a Sign of God's Love. On balance, the type of disdain we feel for this life should not be one of hatred or ingratitude toward God. Even though this world is full of hardship, we must recognize God's kindness in the midst of hard times. He is doing this for our spiritual good—He has our best in mind. To think anything less is to be guilty of complaining and grumbling against Him. After all, God's discipline is proof of His love, given to His children in order to promote their spiritual maturity.

In this way, before openly exhibiting the inheritance of eternal glory, God is pleased to reveal Himself to us in small ways: namely, through the daily blessings that He gives us in this life—including His discipline. Because this life helps acquaint us with the goodness of God, we should not disdain it as though it did not contain one particle of good. We should, rather, appreciate this life for what it is—a gift from God with which we are required to be good stewards. Being quick to remember that it is only momentary, we nonetheless are thankful for what God is teaching us in and through it.

This life gives a preview of God's grace. In witnessing God's goodness here, we can hope in God's goodness for eternity; in experiencing a small foretaste of God's faithfulness on earth, we then look forward to the full manifestation of His faithfulness in heaven. Once we realize that this life is a gift of divine mercy, readying us for the future, we are again drawn to look ahead rather than around— and our excessive fondness for this earth can be exchanged for a proper gratitude to the Savior.

4. You Can Have Hope in Trials Because Trials Cause Us to Long for Eternity. As our love for this world diminishes, our longing for the life to come will increase proportionally. Finding this life full of misery and pain, we make it our aim to push ourselves with utmost effort, without distraction, aspiring to our future and eternal life. After all, this life is nothing compared to the life that is to come. If heaven is our country, what can the earth be but a place of temporary exile?

Of course, we should never hate the life that God has given us here, except that it keeps us subject to sin; and even then, our hatred is not directed against life itself, but against the death that sin has introduced into life. It is actually the sin we battle in this life that causes us to long for its termination. Yet, while we wait, we do so without complaining or impatience. After all, He Himself has assigned us a post—one that we must maintain until He calls us home.

Even the apostle Paul lamented his condition, in being still bound with the prison chains of the body. He longed earnestly for redemption (Romans 7:24). Nonetheless, he declared that, in obedience to the command of God, whether by life or by death, he would do all for God's glory (Philippians 1:20–24). We, too, should despise life because of sin's bondage, longing to leave this earth and be with Christ whenever He so chooses.

Ironically, most Christians do not long for death. Most are so afraid of the thought that they tremble at the very mention of it. Granted, it is understandable that our natural feelings should be somewhat shocked in thinking about death. Yet, the sad reality is that often our fear outweighs our hope. Considering that our present body—an unstable, defective, fading, and temporary tent—must be dissolved in order to be replaced by a perfect, incorruptible, and heavenly body, will faith not compel us to eagerly desire what our nature dreads?

Certainly, we long for immortality. But we will never find immortality here on earth. So we must fix our eyes on heaven, where eternal life is promised. This is what the Scriptures promise! God has taken the horrors of death and turned them into something joyful—where the end of this life is the beginning of eternity. Why is it, then, that what should cause us joy often produces nothing but sadness and anxiety? How can we glory in Him as Master when we pay more homage to our fears than we do to His salvation? Instead, we should long for the day that we will enter into His presence—confidently clinging to the promised inheritance that He freely bestows on all who are His.

A CALL TO HOPEFUL ENDURANCE

As Christians, while we live on this earth, we should be thankful for our trials, knowing that times of hardship conform us into the likeness of Christ (Romans 8:29). In fact, we would be worse off by far if it were not for trials, because trials cause us to look to heaven as we rise above the problems of this life. And, as we raise our heads to see Christ, even though we see the wicked flourishing, we will have no trouble standing firm. After all, our focus will be turned to that future day when we will embrace our Savior, and He will wipe away the tears from our eyes and clothe us in robes of glory.

The hope of heaven, indeed, is our only true consolation in this life. Without it, we will either give way to depression or resort to our own destruction by seeking the things of this world. God sends us trials, then, to keep us on track. With our eyes directed to our Lord and the power of His resurrection, we must live today in light of eternity, rather than squandering eternity for the vanity of today.

CHAPTER 14

YOUR SPIRITUAL BANK ACCOUNT:

The Hope of Finding True Riches in Christ

> *I pray also that the eyes of your heart may be enlightened in order that*
> *you may know the hope to which he has called you,*
> *the riches of his glorious inheritance in the saints.*

EPHESIANS 1:18

Money and material wealth never bring true happiness. This simple fact has been clearly demonstrated time after time. Remember King Solomon? He had more money than he could possibly spend, but by the end of his life, he came to realize it was all vanity. In Ecclesiastes 5:10, he says, "Whoever loves money never has money enough; whoever loves wealth is never satisfied with his income. This too is meaningless."

Other wealthy men throughout history have come to agree with King Solomon. While they expected their riches to bring ultimate happiness, in the end they found nothing but emptiness. For example, it was Andrew Carnegie who reportedly said, "Millionaires seldom smile. Millionaires who laugh are rare. My experience is that wealth is apt to take the smiles away." William Vanderbilt's comment was this: "The care of two hundred million dollars is too great a load for any brain or back to bear. It is enough to kill anyone. There is no pleasure in it." And Henry Ford concluded, "I was happier when doing a mechanic's job."[1]

Even John D. Rockefeller couldn't find happiness in the millions he amassed. When he was asked, "How much is enough?" he answered, "Just a little bit more." Toward the end of his life, he said, "I have made many millions, but they have brought me no happiness. I would barter them all for the days I sat on an office stool in Cleveland and counted myself rich on three dollars a week." And when his accountant was asked, "How much did John D. leave after he died?" The accountant's reply was classic: "He left all of it."[2]

Benjamin Franklin had it right when he said that:

> *Money never made a man happy yet, nor will it. There is nothing in its nature to produce happiness. The more a man has, the more he wants. Instead of it filling a vacuum, it makes one. If it satisfied one want, it doubles and trebles that want another way. That was a true proverb of the wise man; rely upon it: "Better a little with the fear of the Lord, than great treasures."*[3]

President Lincoln's insightful summary was this: "Financial success is purely metallic. The man who gains it has four metallic attributes: gold in his palm, silver on his tongue, brass in his face, and iron in his heart."[4]

God Offers You Lasting Riches

In contrast to the fading wealth of this world, God promises us a lasting inheritance with benefits for both this life and the next. These riches include His kindness and patience (Romans 2:4), His wisdom (Romans 11:33), His grace (Ephesians 2:7), and His mercy (Ephesians 2:4). These resources are infinite (Ephesians 3:8), glorious (Ephesians 3:16), overabundant (Romans 10:12), and truly satisfying because their Source is God Himself (Ephesians 1:18; Philippians 4:19). In reference to our spiritual riches in this life, Pastor John MacArthur says this:

> *Whatever you might be looking for, you can be sure God promised it. God has promised believers peace, love, grace, wisdom, eternal life, joy, victory, strength, guidance, provision for all our needs, power, knowledge, mercy, forgiveness, righteousness, gifts of the Spirit, fellowship with the Trinity, instruction from the Word, truth, spiritual discernment, and eternal riches, to name a few. When we became Christians we were made one with Jesus Christ. Therefore we receive everything the Father gives Him. Paul said we were made "heirs of God, and joint heirs with Christ" (Romans 8:17).*[5]

What a list! And it's not that these are remote possibilities, they are promises. We can hope in these riches because they've been guaranteed by God.

Nowhere in Scripture are these spiritual blessings more clearly laid out than in the first chapter of Ephesians. In fact, in verse three, Paul says that God "has blessed us in the heavenly realms with every spiritual blessing in Christ." In other words, God promises believers infinite spiritual riches and resources—heavenly wealth that will never fade and can never be taken away. Paul continues, in verses 4–14, by listing five specific blessings in which Christians can hope.

1. You Can Hope in God's Choice (Ephesians 1:4). Paul begins his list of spiritual blessings with the fact that God chose us, before we were even born, to be part of His family. In fact, he says, "For he [God, the Father] chose us in him [Christ] before the creation of the world to be holy and blameless in his sight." Imagine that! If we are Christians, we have the joy of knowing that God selected us even before we were alive. Then after we were born, it was God who sought us for Himself. The apostle John states that we can love Him "because he first loved us" (1 John 4:19). And Paul writes that it was God who "made us alive with Christ even when we were dead in transgressions" (Ephesians 2:5).

Of course, God did not choose us because there was anything special about us (1 Corinthians 1:26–29). Instead, it was because of God's grace and for His glory that He chose us. We did not deserve to be chosen. On the contrary, we were headed for hell—the very place we deserved because of our actions. Yet, God rescued us from the path we had made for ourselves.

Not only should God's choice humble us and cause us to worship Him, it should also bring us great comfort. After all, if God chose to save us even when we didn't deserve it, we can be confident that He will complete the work He started in us (see Romans 8:29–30).

2. You Can Hope in God's Grace (Ephesians 1:4–6). Paul continues the list of spiritual riches by speaking of God's immeasurable grace. He writes:

> In love, he [God the Father] predestined us to be
> adopted as his sons through Jesus Christ, in accordance
> with his pleasure and will—to the praise of his glorious
> grace, which he has freely given us in the One he loves.

God could have simply stopped after He chose us. He could have decided to save us from hell and left it at that. But He didn't. Instead, He not only chose to save us, but He made us part of His family—adopting us as His children through Jesus Christ.

All of this, Paul says, is a result of God's grace. In Scripture, grace refers to God's unmerited favor—something that God gives to us even though we do not deserve it. Certainly, our adoption into His family is something we did not deserve and could not earn. It is something He offers simply because He is a gracious Father.

The idea of adoption encompasses numerous spiritual blessings that Christians enjoy. Not only do we now have the hope of a spiritual inheritance (Romans 8:17), but we can also look to God not simply as our Master but also as our Father (Romans 8:15). Whatever our troubles, whether present or future, we can look to Him knowing that He will take care of us as His children (see Matthew 7:9–11).

Our hope, then, is not in an uncaring, unsympathetic, impersonal power. It is in our loving, gracious heavenly Father—the One who, by His grace, selected us to be members of His family through His Son, Jesus Christ.

3. You Can Hope in God's Forgiveness (Ephesians 1:7–8). Not only did God choose us; not only did He adopt us into His family; but He has also forgiven our sins, having redeemed us through the sacrifice of Jesus Christ. Paul notes:

> *In him [Christ] we have redemption through his blood, the forgiveness of sins, in accordance with the riches of God's grace that he lavished on us with all wisdom and understanding.*

Although we deserved punishment, God has granted us pardon. After all, through our sin we had earned nothing but death (Romans 6:23); because of our disobedience, we had fallen far short of God's standard (Romans 3:23)—we were spiritually dead, marked by disobedience and hatred for God (see Ephesians 2:1–3). Yet, because of His mercy and grace, God granted us clemency and gave us spiritual life (Ephesians 2:4–7). Of course, this forgiveness did not come without a price. No, we were redeemed—purchased—at great cost. Jesus Christ, as God the Son, came to earth and paid sin's price with His own life (Romans 8:3). What we could never pay because our debt of sin was too great, God paid for us through the sacrifice of His beloved Son.

Sometimes people worry that God could never forgive them. Maybe they think that their sins are too many, or maybe they fear that one particular sin is too great. But the Bible teaches that no matter how great the offense, God's grace is greater still. His forgiveness knows no end, and He freely grants it to those who humbly and honestly ask. After all, the price Jesus paid for sin, as the infinite and eternal Son of God, is sufficient to cover any wrongdoing. As His children, we hope in His forgiveness, realizing that sin's penalty has been paid and our redemption secured.

4. You Can Hope in God's Wisdom and Purpose (Ephesians 1:9–12). From a worldly standpoint, God's decision to choose us when we were His enemies, to adopt us into His family, and to forgive us our sins might seem somewhat foolish. For starters, we have nothing to offer Him in return. Paul assures us, though, that God has not gone crazy. In fact, His mercy and grace fit perfectly with His infinite wisdom and plan. In light of this, after citing God's wisdom in verse 8, Paul continues in verses 9–12 by saying:

> *And he [God, the Father] made known to us the mystery of his will according to his good pleasure, which he purposed in Christ, to be put into effect when the times will have reached their fulfillment—to bring all things in heaven and on earth together under one head, even Christ. In him we were also chosen, having been predestined according to the plan of him who works out everything in conformity with the purpose of his will, in*

order that we, who were the first to hope in Christ, might be for the praise of his glory.

You see, God is working everything in the universe according to His good pleasure and for His ultimate glory. Paul could not have been any more clear: God's goal is "to bring all things in heaven and on earth together under one head, even Christ. . .for the praise of his glory" (see also 1 Corinthians 15:20–28). Paul's point is that our salvation and spiritual development are part of that plan. This means that everything that happens, including the difficulties we face, is part of God's perfect purpose, a purpose that includes our spiritual good (Romans 8:28).

Certainly, we didn't deserve to be chosen. Nor did we deserve to be adopted into God's family or to have our sins forgiven. Nonetheless, God chose to save us and to redeem us because He has a plan for the universe that includes us. His grace is not bestowed haphazardly; His choice is not random nor are the events He allows in our lives. Because our God is infinitely wise, and because He is in control of all things, we can hope in Him in every situation we face.

5. You Can Hope in God's Guarantee (Ephesians 1:13–14). Paul finishes the list by reminding the Ephesian believers that God has given us His Holy Spirit as a pledge—proving that we are part of His family and guaranteeing that His promises for the future will indeed come true. The apostle writes this:

> *And you also were included in Christ when you heard the word of truth, the gospel of your salvation. Having believed, you were marked in him with a seal, the promised Holy Spirit, who is a deposit guaranteeing our inheritance until the redemption of those who are God's possession—to the praise of his glory.*

By saying "and you also," Paul indicates that all of the spiritual blessings he had received were also given to his readers when they responded to the "gospel of salvation." In fact, these riches have been extended to all who have been "included in Christ." This means that even Christians today can bank on the heavenly wealth described in Ephesians 1.

The proof of these promises is the gift of the Spirit—whom God bestows on all those who are His children. Not only does the Spirit secure the believer's spiritual protection (see chapter 10), but He also certifies the believer's inheritance. While many of God's promises are still future, we can confidently hope in them because God's Spirit ensures that they will come to pass.

REALIZING HOW RICH YOU REALLY ARE

Clearly, our spiritual bank accounts are overflowing with the abundant riches of God. We did not earn the blessings we have received. Yet, God has seen fit to bestow them on us because we are His children— an adoption made possible through the death of Jesus Christ.

How sad it is, then, when Christians forget how rich they really are. Instead of focusing on the true, lasting riches of heaven, they chase after the empty, fading riches of earth. In the end, all the money in the world only has temporal, material value. Like Jesus asks in Matthew 16:26, "What good will it be for a man if he gains the whole world, yet forfeits his soul?" Along these same lines, at the end of his life, Patrick Henry said this:

> *I have now disposed of all my property to my family. There is one thing more I wish I could give them and that is faith in Jesus Christ. If they had that and I had not given them a single shilling, they would have been*

rich; and if they had not that, and I had given them all the world, they would be poor indeed.[6]

CHAPTER 15

WHEN HOPE
COMES BACK FOR YOU:
The Hope of Christ's Return and Reign

For the grace of God that brings salvation has appeared to all men.
It teaches us to say "No" to ungodliness and worldly passions, and to live self-controlled,
upright and godly lives in this present age, while we wait for the blessed hope—
the glorious appearing of our great God and Savior, Jesus Christ,
who gave himself for us to redeem us from all wickedness and to purify for himself
a people that are his very own, eager to do what is good.

TITUS 2:11–14

I imagine it as a sunny morning—just a few clouds in the sky. What a whirlwind the last few weeks had been. Just six weeks ago, the Lord had been wrongly arrested, falsely accused, and unjustly crucified. Peter and the others had thought it was the end, with their dreams and expectations dying on the cross that day, too.

But then, just three days later, Jesus rose from the grave. In the weeks that followed, He appeared to His disciples on numerous occasions, explaining to them why His death had been necessary as the Savior of the world. In fact, the Lord interacted with His followers for forty days after His resurrection, appearing to as many as five hundred at one time. The resulting anticipation was high because the hope that had died on the cross had risen again—there was no longer any room for doubt.

And now, nearly six weeks later, Christ assembled His disciples on the Mount of Olives for one last lesson. As they gathered around Him, He urged them to "go and make disciples of all nations, baptizing them in the name of the Father and of the Son and of the Holy Spirit, and teaching them to obey everything I have commanded you. And surely I am with you always, to the very end of the age" (Matthew 28:19–20). And then, having instructed them to be His witnesses, He ascended into heaven.

Of course, they watched Him as He rose steadily into the air. What a sight that must have been! They watched Him as He disappeared into a cloud. They continued gaping, even after He was gone. And they probably would have gazed into the sky for hours, maybe days, if God had not sent two angels to spur them on their way. "Men of Galilee," said the angels, "why do you stand here looking into the sky? This same Jesus, who has been taken from you into heaven, will come back in the same way you have seen him go into heaven" (Acts 1:11).

With that the disciples dispersed—returning to Jerusalem to wait and pray. Pentecost was only ten days away, meaning that the power of the Holy Spirit would soon enable them to carry out their Lord's commission. Yet, they never forgot the promise of His return. For the rest of their lives, while faithfully attending to the task He had given, the eyes of their hearts continued to look upward—always watching for their hope to be realized in the return of their King.

THE HOPE OF CHRIST'S RETURN

Unlike the disciples, the sad truth is that many Christians today, while claiming ultimate love for their Savior, would prefer that Jesus not return during their lifetime—or, at least, not until the very end. After all, there are so many thrills yet to experience in this life, so many adventures still to be had. If Christ were to come back now, He might interrupt all of these plans and dreams. The common hope, it seems, is that Jesus would delay in order that earthly ends might be pursued.

In contrast, the hope of Christ's coming was of paramount importance for the early church. In fact, its certainty was so real that first-century believers would greet one another with the term "maranatha," meaning "Lord, come quickly." Instead of being frightened by the possibility, they clung to it as the culmination of everything they believed. Not surprisingly, the New Testament reflects this intense anticipation by referencing Jesus' return, whether directly or indirectly, in every New Testament book except Philemon and 3 John.

In the Gospels, the description of the Second Coming is given by Christ Himself. It will be sudden (Matthew 24:27; Luke 17:24), unexpected (Matthew 24:36, 44), and visible in the sky (Mark 14:62); it will include an angelic escort (Mark 8:38) and great power and glory (Mark 13:26; Luke 21:27); it will result in the final redemption of His chosen ones (Luke 21:28); and it is guaranteed by His word (John 14:3, 21:22–23). So, His followers are to keep watch (Matthew 25:13; Mark 13:35; Luke 12:35–47) and live faithfully during His absence (Luke 19:12–26).

The Book of Acts continues this theme. Christ's return will inaugurate His earthly kingdom (1:6) where He will rule as supreme Judge (17:31). In fact, He will come back in the same way He left (1:11), although the time of His coming has not been revealed (1:7).

The epistles also focus the attention of their readers on the imminent return of the Savior. Romans 13:11 commands believers to awake from their spiritual slumber in light of His coming; 1 Corinthians 1:7 and 4:5 encourage Christians to wait on the Lord as they anticipate His return; and 1 Corinthians 15:52 describes just how quickly the events of that day will occur—a day that Paul later calls generally the "day of Christ" (see 2 Corinthians 1:14; Philippians 1:6, 10) and the "day of redemption" (Ephesians 4:30).

Galatians 5:5 tells us we should hope eagerly for it, and Philippians 4:5 suggests that His coming is near. Colossians 3:4 indicates that we will receive our glorified bodies at that very moment, an observation confirmed by 1 Thessalonians 4:13–17. In contrast to the redemption of Jesus' followers, 2 Thessalonians 2:1–12 describes how Christ's return spells out destruction for His enemies. And in 1 Timothy 6:14 and 2 Timothy 4:5, Paul encourages Timothy to live righteously because the Master will soon be back to evaluate the work of His servants.

Titus 2:11–14 calls Christ's coming our "blessed hope," the great climax of history to which all Christians should look with joy and excitement. And Hebrews 10:37 encourages us to remember that our wait will not be too much longer. In the meantime, we are to "be patient" (James 5:7–8) and diligently pursue holiness (1 Peter 1:13, 5:4), rather than doubting His coming (2 Peter 3:3–10) or growing spiritually apathetic (1 John 2:28, 3:2–3). After all, when He appears, believers will be fully rewarded for their faithfulness (2 John 8), while the wicked will be judged (Jude 14–15). So when He says, " 'I am coming soon' " (Revelation 3:11, 22:12, 20), we are to watch for Him with great anticipation. After all, He may even return today.

Clearly, the writers of the New Testament looked to Christ's coming as the source of great comfort and motivation. The same should be true for us today. As God's children, Jesus' arrival from heaven should be our greatest longing and desire. The Bible gives at least four specific reasons why you can hope in Christ's return.

1. You Can Hope in the Fact That Christ Will Return for Certain. The first reason you can have hope in Jesus' return is that it is certain. While we do not know the exact time *when* He will come, we can be confident that He *is* coming. Though the skeptics of the world may mock, equating our hope with science fiction rather than fact (see 2 Peter 3:3–5), we can rest confidently in Christ's promise.

In John 14:3, He told His disciples, "And if I go and prepare a place for you, I will come back and take you to be with me that you also may be where I am." After His resurrection, He reiterated this pledge, repeating it at least four times to the apostle John in the Book of Revelation (3:11, 22:7, 12, 20). As God in human flesh, Jesus' promise is the promise of God Himself. And we can be certain He will make good on what He said.

For confirmation, we can look to the promises God made about Christ's first coming—if Jesus perfectly fulfilled all of the biblical prophecies regarding His first coming, we can be confident that He will do the same regarding His second coming. For example, Jesus was a descendant of David (as foretold in Isaiah 9:6–7), born in Bethlehem (as foretold in Micah 5:2), and born of a virgin (as pictured in Isaiah 7:14). He grew up to bring physical healing and spiritual life (compare Isaiah 61:1–2 with Luke 4:18). He was killed in torture and disdain (as foretold in Isaiah 53:1–12). Yet, He died as the promised sacrifice for sin (as pictured in Genesis 3:15). Many other passages confirm this same conclusion (see Matthew 2:15, 17, 23, 13:14, 35, 26:54, 56, 27:9; Mark 14:49; Luke 1:1, 18:31, 22:37, 24:44; John 17:12, 18:9, 19:24, 28, 36). God kept His word the first time—He'll keep it the next time, too.

2. You Can Hope in the Fact That Christ Will Return for You. As a Christian, you can hope, not only in the fact that Christ will come, but that He's coming for you. As a bridegroom for his bride, Christ will come for His church—a church that includes you and every other believer on earth. Your body will be changed into its perfected and resurrected form (1 Corinthians 15:52). Your heavenly reward will change from hope to reality. Your faith in the Lord will become sight. Your earthly subsistence will be instantly upgraded to eternal vitality.

But what about those who have already died? Are they going to miss out on the joy of Christ's return? Are they not included in these personal promises? These are the exact questions that the church in Thessalonica began asking Paul after several of the members died. Paul, however, allays their fears, assuring them that even those Christians who have already died will be raised to experience the universal, and yet personal, blessings of Jesus' return (1 Thessalonians 4:13–18). Their spirits, having been in heaven with Christ (2 Corinthians 5:8) will return with Him (1 Thessalonians 3:13), where they will receive their resurrection bodies along with those who are still alive on earth. All Christians of all time, then, will participate in their Savior's glorious second coming. No one will be left out.

3. You Can Hope in the Fact That Christ Will Return Soon. As you look forward to Christ's coming, it's easy to begin wondering when it's actually going to happen. After all, it's already been two millennia since the first time He was here. In response, the apostle Peter tells us that it is because of God's great patience that He has waited so long (2 Peter 3:9). Yet, we should guard ourselves against becoming lazy and self-satisfied because the Bible teaches that He could return at any moment.

In the Gospels, Jesus teaches that He will return when no one suspects it (Matthew 24:36, 44). In Romans 13:11, Paul simply reminds us that "our salvation [Jesus' return] is nearer now than when we first believed." This means that, at this exact moment, even as you read this sentence, the Lord's coming is closer in time than ever before. And 1 Corinthians 15:52 indicates the event itself will happen "in a flash, in the twinkling of an eye." So, when Jesus reiterates "I am coming soon" in Revelation 3:11 and 22:20, we should pay attention.

With this in mind, Christians can live hope-filled lives every moment of every day. The trials of life may seem overwhelming, but the Savior is coming back—and soon. The temptations of life may seem irresistible, but the Judge is coming back—and soon. The pain of loss and sickness may seem too great to bear, but the Great Physician is returning—and soon. All who have died will be raised.

All who are alive will be changed. So that, in the end, all Christians will be together with the Lord forever (1 Thessalonians 4:17).

4. You Can Hope in the Fact That Christ Will Return with Power. Christ's appearing will also be significant for unbelievers. Although it is eagerly desired by God's people—because they long for the return of their King—it is equally despised and detested by God's enemies. For them it means punishment and destruction. In fact, 1 Corinthians 15:24–28 indicates that God will put every "dominion, authority and power" under Christ's rule—even death will be defeated. The enemies of the Cross will be crushed, and the earthly reign of Messiah will commence.

Christ's powerful return should give us immense comfort and consolation. The persecution we face as Christians can be endured because the coming King will make things right. And not only that, He promises us that we will rule with Him in His kingdom. As Paul rhetorically asks in 1 Corinthians 6:2, "Do you not know that the saints will judge the world?" Also in 2 Timothy 2:11–12, he says, "Here is a trustworthy saying: If we died with him, we will also live with him; if we endure, we will also reign with him." To think that Christ's earthly rule includes us! (See also Revelation 20:4.) Not only will justice and righteousness prevail, but we get to participate in the process. Even our sanctified imaginations cannot comprehend how glorious this kingdom will be—a kingdom that Jesus will establish at His return.

IT'S TIME TO GET READY

The Bible could not be more plain: Jesus is coming back. It is His promise, so we can believe it is true. It is for His church, so we can eagerly anticipate it. It is imminent, meaning we must be ready at any moment. And it will be with power, meaning that the injustices of this world will end with the installment of Christ Himself.

As His servants, then, we must ask ourselves if we are ready for the return of our Master (Matthew 24:42–51). Have we invested in eternity with the gifts He's given us? Have we been wise stewards of our resources? Have we been diligent to proclaim His message and faithful to live it out? Do we eagerly look forward to His arrival?

It's time for us to get ready. The King is coming, and He is coming soon. As His servants, we should embrace the promise of His return with eagerness, as we wait with patient diligence—working hard so we will not be ashamed when we see Him face-to-face.

CHAPTER 16

PUTTING ON YOUR
BRAND-NEW BODY:
The Hope of Resurrection

By his power God raised the Lord from the dead, and he will raise us also.

1 CORINTHIANS 6:14

I once came across an account of a young New York man diagnosed with an incurable intestinal infection. At twenty-four years of age, Steven was in the prime of his life; he was a poet, a guitarist, a photographer, and an excellent student. Yet, because of his illness, he realized that he only had a few months to live. In light of his situation, Steven decided to have his body frozen at the moment of his death—that way, if a future treatment were ever found, he could be revived and treated, maybe even cured. So, several months before he died, he made all of the necessary arrangements with the Cryonics Society of New York, a group founded on the hypothesis that the bodies of the clinically dead can be frozen and later brought back to life.

When he died, five members of the Cryonics Society promptly took charge, helping a Long Island funeral director pack Steven's corpse in ice cubes for a two-hour drive to the funeral home. There it was drained of its body fluids, and infused with an antifreeze solution to help preserve the body tissues. Then it was packed with dry ice, preparatory to placement in "cryonic suspension" in a "Crypt-Capsule," a giant bottle filled with liquid nitrogen. In that state, Steven will remain indefinitely, maintained at a cost of two hundred dollars per year, an expense paid for out of a Cryonics Trust Fund set up by Steven before his death.[1]

Steven had also discussed his unusual funeral arrangements with his mother, who said that knowing Steven might possibly be revived alleviated some of her pain.

She commented that his death was easier for her to bear because there wasn't the same finality of putting someone away under the earth. She said, "I had talked about it with Steven, not morbidly, just ordinary conversation, and I came to accept the idea." When asked if she expected Steven to be raised from his Cryonic Capsule, she made this tragically significant comment, "I have only a remote hope for my boy's resurrection."[2]

A tragic comment indeed, because her hope was founded in nothing more than the unlikelihood of scientific improbability.

YOUR HOPE OF RESURRECTION

As a Christian, you also have the hope of a future resurrection. But, unlike Steven, your hope is based on the promise of God Himself. It is not the unrealistic dream of science fiction, but rather the future reality of scriptural fact. It requires no ice, no antifreeze, and no liquid nitrogen; in fact, you can be buried, drowned, or cremated—it makes no difference. Instead, all you need is a saving relationship with Jesus Christ. As part of His family you can confidently look forward to what the Bible calls the "resurrection of life" (John 5:29 NKJV). With this in mind, the Bible provides at least three reasons why you can have hope in God's promised resurrection.

1. You Can Hope in Your Future Resurrection Because Christ Already Rose. The primary basis for our hope in a future resurrection is the fact that Christ already rose from the dead. After all, His resurrection is at the heart of everything we believe and look forward to as Christians. If Jesus never conquered death, then everything we are as His followers is a lie (see 1 Corinthians 15:17–19).

The wonderful reality, however, is that Christ has been raised from the dead. And because He has been raised, He is the guarantee of our resurrection (1 Corinthians 15:20–23); because He defeated death, we no longer need to fear it (1 Corinthians 15:26, 55). In fact, the same Spirit that raised Him from the dead is also in us (Romans 8:11), meaning that in Christ we have "the hope of glory" (Colossians 1:27).

Throughout history, the critics, skeptics, and cynics of the world have ridiculed the idea that Jesus actually rose again. Calling it fiction, they claim that the resurrection we celebrate every Easter is actually a farce and a fairy tale. Accordingly, they come up with various theories to explain what really happened on that glorious resurrection morning. Some say Jesus merely swooned on the cross, reviving later in the tomb and proclaiming that He had risen. Others say that He never actually died on the cross, but rather someone else took His place. Still others argue that the disciples either stole the body or experienced some type of mass hallucination. But under scrutiny, all of these allegations fall flat, unable to explain away the historical fact of the matter—that Jesus Christ physically rose from the dead.

The Bible gives us numerous reasons to believe the historical validity of His resurrection. First, the Old Testament prophesied that the Messiah would die and rise again (compare Psalm 16:10 with Acts 2:25–31, 13:33–37; also see Isaiah 53). Second, Jesus Himself predicted His resurrection (Matthew 16:21; Mark 9:9–10; John 2:18–22). Third, even Jesus' enemies knew that He had risen, and therefore they invented a lie as a cover-up (Matthew 28:11–15). Not only that, but His enemies were unable to produce a body, the only thing they would have needed to prove the disciples wrong (John 20:3–9). Fourth, many of Jesus' followers saw Him after He rose (Matthew 28:8–10; Mark 16:9; Luke 24:13–45; John 20:14–29, 21:1–23; Acts 1:3–12, 7:55, 9:3–6, 22:17–21, 23:11; 1 Corinthians 15:5–8; Revelation 1:10–19). At one point, He even appeared to five hundred of them at one time (1 Corinthians 15:3–8). Fifth, the lives of His disciples were inexplicably altered, from cowardly fisherman to courageous preachers (compare Matthew 26:56, 69–75 with Acts 2 and 4). Every one of these men, with the exception of the exiled apostle John, died for their faith. Obviously, they were convinced the resurrection was no fraud. The early church agreed with their leaders, recognizing that the doctrine of the resurrection was central to their faith (Acts 4:33, 5:30–32; Romans 5:21)—so central, in fact, that they also were willing to give up their lives for what they knew to be true.

The predictions of Scripture, the lies of Christ's enemies, the eyewitness sightings of Jesus afterward, and the changed lives of His disciples—it all testifies to the historical reality of the Lord's resurrection. If He did not rise again, then the cynics are right—Christians are fools to believe what they do. But, if He did rise again, and we know that He did, then we can be confident that we will also be raised from the dead.

Paul was so convinced of his own future resurrection that he spoke of it as though it had already happened (see Ephesians 2:6–7). This confidence is echoed in Romans 6:5–9 and Colossians 2:12 where he makes the point that, if we are "in Christ," our resurrection is guaranteed (1 Corinthians 15:22–23). In fact, Paul was so sure of what he believed that he stood trial for it (Acts 24:15) and even gave his life for it. Amazingly, here was man who, at one time had viciously attacked the church (Acts 9:1–2). Yet, having seen the risen Savior on the road to Damascus (Acts 9:3–7), Paul knew that Jesus' resurrection was a historical fact. As a result, he confidently realized that the future resurrection of believers was equally certain.

2. You Can Hope in Your Future Resurrection Because Christ Is Coming Back. Not only has Christ proven that resurrection is possible, by rising from the grave Himself, but He has also given us details as to when our resurrection will take place—namely, at His return (1 Thessalonians 4:14–17). For those believers who are still alive on the earth, their bodies will also be instantly changed into resurrected form at the moment Jesus comes back (1 Corinthians 15:52).

As we saw in chapter 15, Christ's return to earth is a God-guaranteed promise. Paul says, "When Christ, who is your life, appears, then you also will appear with him in glory" (Colossians 3:4). This means that our resurrection is just as certain as Jesus' second coming, since the two events are intertwined. Moreover, our hope of resurrection makes the hope of Christ's return that much sweeter.

In the meantime, God has given us the Holy Spirit as both a guarantee of our spiritual inheritance and the proof of our salvation (see chapter 10). In Romans 8:11, Paul adds an additional aspect of the Spirit's ministry to us. Paul writes, "And if the Spirit of him who raised Jesus from the dead is living in you, he who raised Christ from the dead will also give life to your mortal bodies through his Spirit, who lives in you." In other words, although our bodies are mortal because of sin, yet they will be raised again—given life—by the power of the Spirit who indwells us. What a hope we have, then, as Spirit-filled children of God. Our future bodily resurrection is certain, because of the risen Savior who is coming back for us and because of the Spirit whom God gave us in the meantime.

3. You Can Hope in Your Future Resurrection Because You Will Be Changed. Not only can you look forward to your bodily resurrection with confidence, but with anticipation and excitement, as well. The resurrection is not something to be feared, but something to be eagerly awaited (see 2 Corinthians 5:1–5). Finally, the sins and temptations of this life will be completely gone—our old, wicked flesh having been replaced with a perfect resurrection body (1 Corinthians 15:42–44). We will no longer have any reason to fear pain, sickness, or death (Revelation 21:4) because we will have bodies perfectly suited for eternal life with Christ.

The Bible doesn't tell us exactly how much different our resurrection bodies will be from the bodies we have now. All we have are a few broad details taken from the accounts of Christ after His resurrection. For example, we know that Jesus, in His resurrected form, was recognizable to His followers (although not always immediately—John 20:14, 21:4; Luke 24:31). Also, He was able to eat food (John 21:4–13; Revelation 19:9), even though His new body, being immortal, didn't need food to survive. Jesus could apparently walk through locked doors (John 20:19) and travel great distances very quickly (Luke 24:31). While God's Word is not explicit, it seems our abilities will be similar. Beyond this the details are sketchy. First Corinthians 15:35–44 simply implies that the changes will be significant.

Nonetheless, while not giving us every detail, the Bible does make it clear that our resurrection state will be far better than our current one. In 1 Corinthians 15:47–54, Paul says that we will bear the likeness of Christ Himself—meaning that, when we are raised, we will enjoy the same type of immortal body that Christ has. As a result, we no longer need to fear death, because we serve the One who conquered it. And, on the day He returns, He will give us perfected bodies—bodies that only the Creator Himself could have designed.

LIVING IN LIGHT OF
YOUR FUTURE RESURRECTION

The hope of future resurrection is something no Christian should ever take lightly. After all, it was secured by Christ Himself, through His death on the cross and His resurrection three days later. And, it will be His gift to all believers when He returns to this earth. It guarantees us, as His followers, that we will one day enjoy life as it was meant to be enjoyed—in perfection. Although we deserve eternal torment for our sin, we've been given eternal joy.

When we remember these truths, it helps us keep the things of this life in proper perspective (see Colossians 3:1–2). We can have hope in the midst of temptation, because we look forward to the day when our sinful flesh will no longer be a part of us. We can have hope in the midst of sickness and disease, because even in death we anticipate a better life. We can have hope in the midst of loss, because the Christian friends and family whom we've buried will one day rise again. And, instead of clinging so desperately to the things of this life, we can let them go, because we know what the future holds.

Although he did not claim to be born again, Benjamin Franklin actually articulated the hope of future resurrection better than many Christians do today. With his usual humorous wit, Franklin wrote this in his own epitaph:

> *The Body of B. Franklin, Printer*
> *Like the Cover of an old Book*
> *Its contents torn out,*
> *And stript of its Lettering and Gilding,*
> *Lies here, Food for Worms,*
> *But the Work shall not be wholly lost:*
> *For it will, as he believ'd,*
> *Appear once more*

In a new & more perfect Edition,
Corrected and amended by the Author.

If only the church today would share just a little of Franklin's perspective. Sure, cosmetic sales might drop, clothing stores might suffer, and weight-loss manuals might not be best-sellers. But wouldn't it be great if we stopped worrying so much about these temporal bodies we have now and started thinking in terms of eternity. After all, one day you'll have a brand-new body and a glorious eternity to spend enjoying it.

CHAPTER 17

THE ULTIMATE REUNION:

*The Hope of Spending Eternity with
Christ, Family, and Friends*

*Brothers, we do not want you to be ignorant about those who
fall asleep, or to grieve like the rest of men, who have no hope.
We believe that Jesus died and rose again and so we believe that
God will bring with Jesus those who have fallen asleep in him. . . .
And so we will be with the Lord forever.*

1 THESSALONIANS 4:13–14, 17

Family reunions were an important part of my life growing up. Because my immediate family lived in California while the rest of our relatives were in Kansas, we were only able to visit them once each year—usually around Christmas. Thankfully, both sets of grandparents lived within three miles of each other, so our annual trek only required one stop.

As you can imagine, our trips to Kansas were activity packed from the time we arrived until the time we left. There were two sets of cousins to visit, two family Christmases to celebrate, numerous presents to open, and countless meals to eat. Of course, my dad would sit in the living room with all of the uncles, catching up on everything that had happened in the previous months. And my mom would mingle with all of my aunts, usually in the kitchen, as they prepared more food than could possibly be consumed. As for me and my brother, we would go downstairs to the basement and play games with the cousins—laughing and joking as though we had been in Kansas the entire time.

At the end of our visit, we would pack up the car and mentally prepare ourselves for the twenty-three-hour journey back home. We would say our good-byes, exchange the appropriate hugs, and then we'd be off. And while we certainly loved the family we were leaving behind, the parting was never overly sad or sorrowful because we knew we'd be back next Christmas—eager to see everyone again.

In a similar sense, God has also planned a future reunion for His family. Although death separates us from the earthly family and friends we love, the separation is only temporary. Not only that, but once we are reunited in heaven, we will never be separated again. Certainly, death is still painful, but as Christians we can rest confidently in the fact that the loneliness will not last forever. Heaven will reunite us as we worship God together in the presence of our Savior.

Here are three reasons you can look forward to the ultimate family reunion:

1. You Can Hope in Knowing You Will See Your Savior. While heaven will certainly include being reunited with fellow Christians, its primary joy will stem from finally being face-to-face with Christ Himself. All this long life, we may fellowship with Him through prayer and His Word. We may know the peace He brings, we may trust His wisdom, and we may witness His power. Yet, our joy will never be complete until we are with Him in person, when faith becomes sight and hope becomes reality (see Philippians 1:23–24).

In Ephesians 2:6–7, Paul says that Christians will be seated with Christ in heaven, meaning that our relationship with Him will be one of both honor and permanence. In fact, one of the reasons Christ died was so that we could live with Him forever (1 Thessalonians

5:10). The apostle John, in Revelation 19:6–9, highlights just how wonderful an eternity spent with Christ will be by comparing it to a wedding celebration. What better picture could have been chosen? There is nothing more wonderful on this earth than when a young man and a young woman begin their lives together, promising themselves to one another, and embarking upon the most intimate relationship they will ever know. Yet, in heaven, the celebration will be even more wonderful. Our life together with Christ will never end. The promise that He gives to us will never be broken. And the intimate fellowship we share with Him will be infinitely deeper than anything we can know in this life.

In fact, all of our joy in heaven will find its source in Christ Himself and in our relationship with our Savior. J. I. Packer sums it up like this:

> *We cannot visualize heaven's life and the wise man will not try to do so. Instead we will dwell on the doctrine of heaven, where the redeemed will find all their heart's desire: joy with their Lord, joy with His people, and joy in the ending of all frustration and distress and in the supply of all wants. What was said to the child—"If you want sweets and hamsters in heaven, they'll be there"—was not an evasion but a witness to the truth that in heaven no felt needs or longings go unsatisfied. What our wants will actually be, however, we hardly know, except the first and foremost: We shall want to be "always. . .with the Lord" (1 Thessalonians 4:17).*
>
> *What shall we do in heaven? Not lounge around but worship, work, think, and communicate, enjoying activity, beauty, people, and God. First and foremost, however, we shall see and love Jesus, our Savior, Master, and Friend.[1]*

To know that we will one day look into the eyes of the One who died for us, the One whom we worship and serve—the thought is breathtaking. Death is no longer an end, but a beginning—the doorway to the Savior. It was George MacDonald who said, "We seek not death, but still we climb the stairs where death is one wide landing to the rooms above." It is much easier to climb those stairs, knowing that Christ is waiting at the top.

In fact, heaven is only heaven because God is there. I have sometimes heard Christians wonder out loud if heaven will be boring. After all, eternity is a very long time. Will it ever grow tiresome or dull? The answer, of course, is no—because the essence of heaven is not a place, but a Person. And just as our fellowship with Christ grows sweeter and sweeter in the progress of this life, so it will be in the next. And because our Lord is infinite, an eternity will never exhaust the wonder of knowing Him.

Heaven will never grow wearisome because knowing Christ will never get old. Every moment of eternity will focus on Him, without interruption or diffusion. In worshiping Him forever, we will experience nothing less than everlasting joy—the culmination of the relationship we enjoy with Him currently. With this in mind, as we journey through this life, we can be encouraged to know that one day we will see the Savior whom we love.

2. You Can Hope in Knowing You Will See All the Biblical Saints. Although being with Christ would surely be enough, our hope also includes the promise of fellowshipping with all of God's people of all time. Hebrews 11 mentions just a few of the biblical saints whom we will join in heaven: Abel, Enoch, Noah, Abraham, Sarah, Isaac, Jacob, Moses, Rahab, the Judges, David, Samuel, and the prophets. Have you ever imagined what questions you might ask Noah? Or what your conversation with Elijah might include?

Jesus Himself says in Matthew 8:11, "I say to you that many will come from the east and the west, and will take their places at the feast with Abraham, Isaac and Jacob in the kingdom of heaven." Who do you think you'll sit by in the halls of heaven? Maybe Peter or Moses or Isaiah. And these are just a few of the myriad saints who will be present. There will be Israelites there who walked between walls of water when God parted the Red Sea. There will be priests there who offered sacrifices to inaugurate Solomon's temple. There will be Jews who were part of the Babylonian captivity along with early church saints who were martyred for their faith. There will be men and women from every stage of history, all present as trophies of God's grace. And in each conversation, though the details will be different and the circumstances unique, the theme will be the same: "Give God the glory for His working in my life."

What a wonderful family reunion it will be when all of the members of God's family are assembled. We will all be perfectly righteous, so there will be no petty bickering or sibling rivalry. We will all have glorified bodies, so there will be no hint of self-consciousness or inadequacy. And we will all be focused on Christ, meaning that we will worship Him as one great choir—a choir that includes the angels and every saint who has ever lived.

3. You Can Hope in Knowing You Will See Departed Family and Friends. Seeing Abraham, Ezekiel, John the Baptist, and all the other biblical saints is going to be remarkable. But for many of us, the hope of seeing our departed loved ones is even more wonderful. An unknown author put it like this:

> *As a boy, I thought of heaven as a city with domes, spires, and beautiful streets, inhabited by angels. By and by my little brother died, and I thought of heaven much as before, but with one inhabitant that I knew. Then another died, and then some of my acquaintances, so in time I began to think of heaven as containing several people that I knew. But it was not until one of my own*

little children died that I began to think I had treasure in heaven myself. Afterward another went, and yet another. By that time I had so many acquaintances and children in heaven that I no more thought of it as a city merely with streets of gold but as a place full of inhabitants. Now there are so many loved ones there I sometimes think I know more people in heaven than I do on earth.[2]

Because God has promised a heavenly home to all of His children, we can be confident that we will be reunited with our Christian parents, siblings, children, and friends who have died. From the godly grandparent we never knew to the believing son or daughter who died much earlier than expected, they are all waiting for us to join them on the other side of death. F. B. Meyer understood this tremendous reality. Just a few days before his death, he wrote a close friend with these words: "I have just heard, to my great surprise, that I have but a few days to live. It may be that before this reaches you, I shall have entered the palace [of heaven]. Don't trouble to write. We shall meet in the morning."[3]

This hope has been the expectation of God's people throughout all of history, including the believers of the early church.

Around A.D. 125, a Greek by the name of Aristeides wrote to one of his friends, trying to explain the extraordinary success of the new religion, Christianity. In his letter he said, "If any righteous man among the Christians passes from this world, they rejoice and offer thanks to God, and they accompany his body with songs and thanksgiving as if he were setting out from one place to another nearby."[4]

Instead of weeping like those who have no hope of ever being reunited (1 Thessalonians 4:13–18), these early Christians under-stood that they would see one another again. They also realized that the believer who dies goes to be with Jesus. Suddenly, when viewed from that perspective, the funeral becomes a celebration rather than a dirge. There are no absolute good-byes in Christianity, just see-you-laters. And when that future day comes, when we will all be reunited, it will be even better than before—because our hearts will be new, our home will be new, and our Savior will be with us to make our joy complete.

TOGETHER FOREVER

Believers should take comfort in knowing they will spend eternity with their Savior and all of His saints. As the community of the re-deemed, we will sing as one great choir—worshiping God for the mercy He has shown us through His Son.

Though our believing friends and family leave us in this life, their absence is only for a little while—at the most, a few short years. And then we will be reunited, this time to experience together the heavenly splendors of our eternal home. In all of this, the Savior who promises to never leave or forsake us will be by our side—ready to welcome us home when our travels on earth are over.

A story is told about the hymn writer, Fanny Crosby, who lost her sight when she was only six months old. On one occasion a sym-pathetic preacher told Fanny, "I think it is a great pity that the Master did not give you sight when He showered so many other gifts upon you."

Without hesitation, Fanny quickly replied, "Do you know that if at birth I had been able to make one petition, it would have been that I should be born blind?"

"Why?" asked the startled cleric.

"Because when I get to heaven, the first face that shall ever gladden my sight will be that of my Savior!"[5]

Some years later, at the age of ninety-five, Fanny's dream came true when she quietly left this earth and went home to see her Lord.

Think of it, Fanny Crosby is in heaven right now, as you read this sentence. With sight she never had while on this earth, she is looking upon her Savior in worship and adoration. With her are thousands of others—some of whom you may even know personally. And the center of it all is Christ. One day you will be there, too, celebrating with your spiritual family for all eternity.

CHAPTER 18

THE ULTIMATE REFLECTION:

The Hope of Being like Christ

Dear friends, now we are children of God,
and what we will be has not yet been made known.
But we know that when he appears, we shall be like him, for we shall see him as he is.

1 JOHN 3:2

Perhaps you remember the television ad campaign with the slogan "I want to be like Mike," namely, Michael Jordan the basketball legend. The idea behind the commercial was clear enough: If you purchase the product, you will be that much more like Michael Jordan. After all, he used the product. . .for at least thirty seconds on television.

For Christians, we have a similar slogan—although it doesn't involve either Mr. Jordan or the products he endorses. That slogan is this: "I want to be like Christ." Of course, there are limits on the scope of this statement. Certainly, we do not imitate Him exactly—by walking on water or claiming to be the Messiah. Yet, we long to be conformed to His image, to be clothed in His righteousness, to be worthy of His name, and to gain His approval.

While we strive for Christlikeness even in this earth, our hopes of being like Him will never be fully realized until His second coming. Even those who have already died and are in heaven still await the culmination of this promise—because they await their resurrection bodies. And they will not receive these new bodies until Christ returns (see chapter 16).

In Romans 8:29, the Holy Spirit through Paul establishes the fact that we can hope in one day being like Christ. After all, it is God's promise. He says, "For those God foreknew he also predestined to be conformed to the likeness of his Son, that he might be the firstborn among many brothers." (See also 1 Corinthians 15:48–49 and Philippians 3:20–21.)

Certainly there are different aspects to this transformation, as will be discussed in this chapter. Yet, the change is a process that begins in this life and is finally fully realized when He returns and we receive our resurrection bodies (see 2 Corinthians 3:18). We reflect Him more and more as we grow in righteousness (1 Corinthians 11:1; 1 John 4:17). But we will not reflect Him perfectly until we have been made completely righteous and been given a resurrection body that is made in His likeness.

Charles Spurgeon (1834–1892) was a man who longed to be conformed into the image of his Savior. Having begun his preaching career at only twenty years of age, Spurgeon quickly became known for his high commitment to Scripture and his excellent oratory. Often, he would preach to audiences with as many as ten thousand listeners, all without electronic amplification, earning him the title "The Prince of Preachers."

Imagine yourself in the audience one Sunday. The year is 1855 and the date May 20. You sit there silently, captivated by every word of Spurgeon's eloquence and conviction. The message this morning comes from Psalm 17:15, a verse that Spurgeon reads aloud: "As for me, I will see Your face in righteousness; I shall be satisfied when I awake in Your likeness" (NKJV). And as he preaches this psalm, in a sermon that I have adapted below, your mind clings to five sure reasons that you can hope in one day being like your Savior.

A MESSAGE OF HOPE FROM CHARLES SPURGEON

1. You Can Hope in Being like Christ Because He Is the Right Focus. When we eagerly anticipate the fact that we will one day be like Christ, we automatically take our eyes off of this world and put them on Him. The wicked around us—in the context of Psalm 17— may seem successful and satisfied in their affluence and self-indulgence. They seemed successful, in an earthly sense, to the psalmist as well. Yet, David does not envy the wicked because he realizes that the happiness of this earth pales when compared with the joy of knowing the Lord and being conformed into His image.

Not only does the hope of being like Christ take our eyes off of the temporal, but in so doing it puts our eyes on the eternal. This is, in fact, David's claim because he uses the future tense, "I will," in referring to this hope. The psalmist looks beyond the grave into another world; he overlooks the narrow deathbed where he has to sleep, and he says, "when I awake." How happy are those with an eye to the future! This must be the perspective of the Christian. Ask for no royal pomp or fame now; be prepared to wait—endure until we get our reward in heaven, the glorious reward that God has provided for those who love Him. We can be content with a small abode in the present, for one day we will have a mansion from God.

Do you know what it is to live looking toward the future, to live in expectation, to live on what you will have in the next world? Do you know what it is to feast upon droppings of the tree of life that fall from heaven, to live upon the manna of expectation which falls in the wilderness, and to drink from the stream of nectar that gushes from the throne of God? Have you ever gone to the great Niagara of hope, and drunk the spray with ravishing delight; that wondrous spray of heaven is glorious to the soul! This is the greatest motivation anyone can have, living in light of the future; seeking nothing here, but expecting that we will shine when we awake in the likeness of Jesus—ready to worship and adore our Savior and Lord.

2. You Can Hope in Being like Christ Because It Is His Promise. Not only does the psalmist have an eye toward the future, but he is also confident in the fact that he will one day awake in the likeness of his Savior. He was full of faith—the psalm itself exudes confidence. "As for me," says David with no doubt about it, "I *will* see Your face in righteousness; I *shall* be satisfied when I awake in Your likeness."

Sadly, there are many who think it is impossible for anyone to know anything with absolute certainty. Yet, there are thousands and thousands of God's people alive in the world right now who can say with total confidence, "I *will* see Your face in righteousness; I *shall* be satisfied when I awake in Your likeness."

What a happy thing to have a faith that says "I *will!*" What a glorious thing to have the confidence of assurance, so that at the end of your life you can say, "I *will* see Your face; I *shall* be satisfied when I awake in Your likeness." Imagine yourself on your deathbed. You only have days, maybe only hours, to live. At that point in life, the riches of this earth will mean nothing to you. The only solace you will have is the blessed assurance of faith in Jesus Christ—a faith founded in His promise that those who are His will one day be like Him.

3. You Can Hope in Being like Christ with Regard to Righteousness. But what will this likeness include? What does it mean that we will be like Christ? Well, first of all, we will be like Him in regard to righteousness—meaning that we will be perfect, just as He is perfect. With this in mind, David says, "I will see God's face in righteousness."

Have I not seen my Father's face here below? Yes, I have, "through a glass darkly." There is so much sin to darken the eyes, so much folly, so much frailty, that we do not yet have a clear picture of our Lord. Nonetheless, when that glorious day comes, and we see our Savior face-to-face, we will see Him "in righteousness." Christians in heaven will not have so much as a speck upon their garment; they will be pure and white. Although we have been washed in His blood, our righteousness will not be totally apparent until heaven.

Our righteousness is sometimes smoked by earth and covered with dust from this carnal world; but in heaven it will have been polished and washed clean. After all, we will be clothed in the robes of Jesus' righteousness—a righteousness free of blemish or stain. Although only perfect righteousness can see God, we will enjoy that privilege—not because of any merit on our behalf, but because of the righteousness Christ gives us. We can hope in being like Him because we will share in His perfection.

4. You Can Hope in Being like Christ with Regard to Your Satisfaction. Not only does being like Christ include receiving His righteousness, it includes our total satisfaction. After all, in heaven everything takes place in perfect conformity to Christ's desires. In being made like Him, we will be in perfect agreement with those desires—meaning that as they are fulfilled, we will be satisfied.

For this reason, heaven is the home of true and real satisfaction. Believers will be so satisfied there, with all of God's will, that we will praise God for the mercies of heaven and even glorify Him for the justice of hell. In heaven we will think rightly of both God and mankind. Here people sometimes seem to be great things to us; but in heaven they will seem to be no more than the insects that are swept away in plowing a field for harvest; they will seem like such little things when we sit on high with God, look down on the nations of the earth as grasshoppers, and "count the islands as very little things."

We will be satisfied with everything, because our wants will be in perfect harmony with the Savior. His desires for us will be the very desires we have, because we will have been changed into His likeness. There will be nothing to cause us to complain.

5. You Can Hope in Being like Christ with Regards to Your Resurrection Body. Not only will we be like Christ in terms of our righteousness and our thinking, but also in our resurrection body. Even those who are in heaven now have not fully been made into the likeness of Christ. Not until the future resurrection will believers—including those who have already died—receive the same type of body their Savior already possesses.

When David says, "I will awake in the likeness of God," he includes the aspect of bodily resemblance—because "awaking" carries with it the idea of resurrection. What a thought! The body is to be in the likeness of Christ. We can only imagine what Christ is like—physically. He is described in Scripture as bright and glorious; His eyes are like lamps of fire; His tongue like a two-edged sword; His head is covered with hair as white as snow, for He is the Ancient of Days, and when He speaks, it is like the sound of rushing water! We can read the accounts given in the book of Revelation, but we cannot fully understand their meaning. Whatever they mean, we do know that we will wake up in Christ's likeness. What a change it will be when we get to heaven!

Imagine a man who fell in battle but not before God saved him. His legs had been shot away, and his body had been scarred by sword thrusts. Yet, he wakes in heaven and finds that he no longer has a broken body; he is not maimed or injured; he is in Christ's likeness.

Imagine an old widow, who has tottered on her crutch for many years along her weary way; time has ploughed furrows on her brow; haggard and lame, her body is laid in the grave. This woman will arise in beauty—in Christ's likeness.

Whatever we may have looked like in this life, whatever our shape or features, our hope for the next life is a resurrection body fashioned in the likeness of Christ. Those who shone on earth, peerless, among the most beautiful, who ravished men with looks from their eyes, they will be no brighter in heaven than those who are now overlooked and neglected—for they will all be like Christ.

THE HOPE OF CHRISTLIKENESS IS FOR ALL WHO ARE SAVED

As with all of the promises of God's Word, the hope of being like Christ is only valid for those who belong to Him. And what a sweet hope it is, allowing us to focus on Him rather than on the passing riches of this world. After all, He has given us His Word—to which we can confidently cling. To think that we will one day be completely righteous as Christ is righteous, that we will think in accordance with Christ's mind, and that we will have a resurrection body not unlike Christ's body—these are just some of the pillars of our hope.

As Christians, we should live each day in light of our glorious hope, remembering that heaven is our home. In the present, we are there only in faith. But in the future, we will be there in body and spirit, when we wake up in God's likeness.

CHAPTER 19

YOUR HEAVENLY MANSION:
The Hope of Christ's Reward

"In my Father's house are many rooms;

if it were not so, I would have told you.

I am going there to prepare a place for you.

And if I go and prepare a place for you,

I will come back and take you to be with me that you also may be where I am."

JOHN 14:2–3

All through the New Testament, the promise of heavenly reward is given as a motivation to Christian faithfulness. In Matthew 16:24–27, Jesus tells His disciples that those who deny themselves, for His sake, will be rewarded with everlasting life (see also Matthew 5:10). This heavenly anticipation is heightened by the parable of the slaves in Luke 19:11–27, in which each servant was rewarded according to the level of his faithfulness.

In the epistles, 1 Corinthians 3:13–15 speaks of the eternal reward that faithful Christian leaders will receive. Second Corinthians 5:10 extends this to all believers, noting that we will be given our reward before the judgment seat ("bema" seat) of Christ (see also

Romans 14:10). Ephesians 6:8 says that the Lord will "reward everyone for whatever good he does." And the author of Hebrews tells his audience that they will be richly rewarded for their faithful endurance (Hebrews 10:34–35) and for their rejection of sinful pleasures (Hebrews 11:24–26).

Scripture uses several different metaphors when speaking of the believer's reward. Matthew 6:20 calls our reward "treasures in heaven" that we should be busy storing up. In Luke 19:11–27 the reward is compared to money. In John 14:2–3, it is pictured as a mansion, or a room in God's house. Even more frequently, our reward is described as a crown. James speaks of the "crown of life" (James 1:12; see Revelation 2:10), Peter of the "crown of glory" (1 Peter 5:4), and Paul of the "crown of righteousness" (2 Timothy 4:8), and of "a crown that will last forever" (1 Corinthians 9:25). Revelation 4:4 also speaks of "crowns of gold" noting that those in heaven "lay their crowns before [Christ's] throne" (Revelation 4:10).

Metaphors aside, the actual reward may involve positions of authority within Christ's eternal kingdom (see Matthew 25:21, 23). Whatever the case, the motivation for personal faithfulness is clearly prescribed. As George Mueller's biographer aptly notes:

> *Christians do not practically remember that while we are saved by grace, altogether by grace, so that in the matter of salvation works are altogether excluded; yet that so far as the rewards of grace are concerned, in the world to come, there is an intimate connection between the life of the Christian here and the enjoyment and the glory in the day of Christ's appearing.*[1]

Some will protest that the use of future reward as an incentive for faithfulness introduces alternative and selfish motives into the Christian life. This is simply not the case because God Himself offers it to us as a motivation. After all, the reward is simply an extension of the reward Giver. To desire His reward is, in the end, to desire His approval and, therefore, to desire to please and glorify Him. On the other hand, to despise what He offers as an incentive is, ultimately, to despise Him—inferring that His reward is less than just.

God does not offer us rewards because He is so obligated, but because He loves us. Even our faithfulness is only possible by His grace. In light of this, we should respond with thanksgiving for the rewards He offers, finding in them renewed motivation to please Him as our King. As Jesus Himself says, "Behold, I am coming soon! My reward is with me, and I will give to everyone according to what he has done" (Revelation 22:12).

Jonathan Edwards (1703–1758) knew what it was to look forward to heaven for his reward. After serving for nearly twenty-five years at his church in Northampton, New Jersey, he was forced to resign by his own people, primarily because he took a firm stand on biblical truth. Not willing to give up, he continued to minister in Stockbridge, Massachusetts, to congregations of both Indian natives and European settlers until his death in 1758.

As with Spurgeon in the previous chapter, imagine yourself in Edwards's congregation. It is Christmas Day, 1737. The title of the message is "Many Mansions" and the text is John 14:2: "In my Father's house are many rooms [mansions]; if it were not so, I would have told you. I am going there to prepare a place for you." The rest of this chapter is adapted from Edwards's sermon. Listen as he gives you four reasons to hope in your heavenly mansion, or reward.

A Message of Hope from Jonathan Edwards

1. You Can Hope in Your Heavenly Mansion Because Christ Is Preparing It for You. Having told His disciples that He was about to leave them, Jesus comforted them by assuring them that He was going to His Father's house—and that one day they, too, would come to that same place. For in the Father's house there are many rooms, enough for Christ as well as His followers.

When the disciples realized that Jesus was going away, they obviously wanted to go with Him, especially Peter. Peter had earlier asked Christ where He was going because Peter wanted to follow Him there. When Jesus told him that he could not follow now, but that he had to wait until later, Peter was not satisfied. "Lord," he said, "why can't I follow you now?" (John 13:37). His desire was representative of the entire group of disciples; they loved their Master and they longed to stay with Him. For this reason, Christ encouraged them that they would be reunited in due time, because in His Father's house were many mansions. There was a mansion for Him, there were mansions for them, and there are mansions for all Christians throughout history. In fact, the reason Jesus left was so that He might prepare a place for them, that it might be ready for them when they followed.

2. You Can Hope in Your Heavenly Mansion Because It Is Part of God's House. The mansions that Christ promised are said to be in His Father's house, namely heaven. Heaven is represented in Scripture as God's dwelling place. Psalm 113:5 asks, "Who is like the LORD our God, the One who sits enthroned on high?" And Psalm 123:1 states, "I lift up my eyes to you, to you whose throne is in heaven." Heaven is God's palace. It is the house of the great King of the universe; it is where He has His throne (Psalm 11:4).

Heaven is not only the place where God has His throne; it is also where He keeps His table, so to speak. It is where His children sit down with Him in His banquet hall to enjoy a royal feast becoming the children of so great a King. It is the dwelling place of all who are in His household (Ephesians 2:19). In Luke 22:30, Jesus said, "that you may eat and drink at my table in my kingdom," and in Matthew

26:29, He promises, "I will not drink of this fruit of the vine from now on until that day when I drink it anew with you in my Father's kingdom."

God is the King of kings, and heaven is the place where He keeps His court. There are His angels and archangels who are the nobles of His court—His attendants. To think that part of our reward includes a place in His house is too wonderful to even comprehend.

3. You Can Hope in Your Heavenly Mansion Because It Is Part of Your Reward. When Jesus said to His disciples, "In My Father's house are many mansions," (John 14:2 NKJV), He implies that there are different degrees and circumstances of honor and reward even in heaven. In other words, there are many rooms in God's house because heaven is intended for various degrees of honor. Some mansions are built in higher places than others; some are designed to have more distinction and glory than others. Although they are all mansions of exceeding honor and blessedness, in which every person will find perfect happiness, some are more distinguished than others.

This, of course, is how any palace is built. While every part of the palace is magnificent, there are nonetheless some apartments that are nicer than others and some more stately and costly than others, according to the degree of dignity. There is one apartment that is the king's presence-chamber; another for the next heir to the crown; there are others for other children; and others for their attendants and the great officers of the household: one for the high steward, another for the chamberlain, and others for lesser officers and servants.

It's not that we are to understand Jesus' words in a strictly literal sense, such that every saint in heaven will possess a certain room where he or she will be physically located. It is not Christ's intent in this passage to inform us much about the external or spatial details of heaven. Rather, we are to understand what Christ says chiefly in a spiritual sense.

People in heaven will receive different degrees of honor and glory, as is abundantly manifested in Scripture—a truth that Christ illustrates by referring to the different mansions or apartments that make up a king's palace. Some rooms will be nearer the throne than others. Some will sit next to Christ in glory, as Matthew 20:23 makes clear, "To sit at my right or left is not for me to grant. These places belong to those for whom they have been prepared by my Father." So, while every believer will inherit the kingdom (and be infinitely happy therein), not every believer will receive the same degree of reward.

4. You Can Hope in Your Heavenly Mansion Because It Will Last Forever. In light of the fact that God gives different degrees of reward for our faithfulness on this earth, we must look to the things of heaven and build up treasure there, rather than in this world. After all, the rewards of this life are only temporary. The mansions of this world will not last forever. In a very short time, you will vacate the earthly house that you now occupy. No matter how grand your current mansion, it is but a tent that will soon be taken down and discarded. Your stay here is, as it were, but for a night. So put your stock in what will last, knowing that Christ will reward you for your obedience.

The mansions in God's house are everlasting mansions. Those who have rooms given to them there, whether of greater or lesser dignity, will keep them for all eternity (Revelation 3:12). If you think it is important to get a good seat in church on Sunday morning, how much more important is it to seek a high reward in heaven! Concern yourself with taking every opportunity for faithfulness—so that you might have a distinguished and glorious mansion in God's heavenly house.

With this in mind, the main thing that we prize in God's house must not be the reward itself, but the One who gives it—because it is with our motives and our hearts that God is pleased. And spend your time here on this earth seeking Christ—that He might prepare a place for you in His Father's house, so that when He comes again to this world, He may take you to Himself, that where He is, there you may be also.

CHAPTER 20

HEAVEN'S R & R:

The Hope of Rest and Reverence in Heaven

There remains, then, a Sabbath-rest for the people of God;
for anyone who enters God's rest also rests from his own work,
just as God did from his.

HEBREWS 4:9–10

Have you ever wondered what will primarily occupy your time when you are in heaven? The keyhole of Scripture gives us only brief glimpses into our heavenly homeland. What the Bible does tell us, however, indicates that at least two basic activities will consume most, if not all, of our heavenly stay—namely, rest and worship. Yet, with both of these activities, their heavenly version is far different than the earthly stereotype.

Heavenly rest is not laziness or lethargy; it is not sitting on a cloud strumming a harp; nor is it the boredom some associate with eternity. It is rest from the burdens, trials, and temptations of this world. Sin and death will be no more, so we can rest from our troubles while also resting in Christ's love. The apostle John, in discussing this rest, says this: "Then I heard a voice from heaven say, 'Write: Blessed are the dead who die in the Lord from now on.' 'Yes,' says the Spirit, 'they will rest from their labor, for their deeds will follow them'" (Revelation 14:13). In other words, heavenly rest is a rest from hardship—from a place of temporal affliction to a place of permanent peace (2 Corinthians 5:1–8). It is an extension, in heavenly form, of the very rest that Christ offers in Matthew 11:28. But it is not, in any sense, a state of glorified laziness or complete inactivity.

Similarly, heavenly worship will not be the dry, ethereal ritualism that many imagine. Instead, it will be the vibrant overflow of our joy—the triumphant response of all believers to God's blessings in salvation (Revelation 4:11, 5:9). C. S. Lewis explains why our heavenly worship will not feel forced but will be the high point of our heavenly experience:

> *We delight to praise what we enjoy because the praise not merely expresses but completes the enjoyment; it is its appointed consummation. If it were possible for a created soul fully to "appreciate," that is, to love and delight in, the worthiest object of all, and simultaneously at every moment to give this delight perfect expression, then that soul would be in supreme blessedness. To praise God fully we must suppose ourselves to be in perfect love with God, drowned in, dissolved by that delight which, far from remaining pent up within ourselves as incommunicable bliss, flows out from us incessantly again in effortless and perfect expression. Our joy is no more separable from the praise in which it liberates and utters itself than the brightness a mirror receives is separable from the brightness it sheds.[1]*

Our praise to God is essentially a natural extension of our love for God. Because our love will be perfect in heaven, so will our praise. And because our joy is intrinsically tied to that which we praise, our joy will also be perfect. In worshiping Him, we will fully delight in Him. And, because He is wholly worthy of praise, being infinite in His perfection, our delight will be equally infinite, resulting in our own inexpressible exuberance. So, our heavenly worship will not be a strain or a duty but rather the source of our eternal joy—our eternal nourishment and happiness. As a result, we will be totally satisfied, knowing greatest pleasure, because our delight is in God Himself. To delight in anything else, while not only being false worship, is to ultimately end up disappointed, because only God can satisfy.

Our perspective on life will necessarily change once we understand the rest and worship of heaven. Suddenly, an earthly retirement is not so important because heavenly rest is waiting. We can spend our entire lives devoted to His work, knowing that there will be plenty of time to catch our breath after this life is over. Also, we will be again reminded that the things of this earth can never satisfy us. Just as God will be our satisfaction and delight in heaven, so He should be here. Until we prize Him above everything else, giving Him our praise and our worship, we will never understand the joy of the Lord. Nor will we really comprehend how wonderful heaven is, especially since worship is its fundamental pastime.

This was the very outlook of Richard Baxter (1615–1691), a well-known Puritan pastor and author. In his book *The Saints' Everlasting Rest,* Baxter discusses the hope of our eternal rest and the never-ending praise we will give God as a result. Baxter wrote this work while he was deathly ill and far from home, with no study tools except his Bible. For many months, he expected that he might die at any moment. As a result, he turned his attention to the topic of heaven, a subject he later said benefited him more than all the other studies of his life. The next few pages contain snapshots of Baxter's heavenward focus.[2] As you read them, remember that our heavenly rest and our heavenly worship go hand in hand. After all, in freeing us up from the temptations and trials of this world, our promised rest will enable us to focus fully on our Savior, Jesus Christ.

A Message of Hope from Richard Baxter

Pray daily and meditate upon your heavenly future. Lay aside all worldly thoughts, and with all possible seriousness and reverence, look to heaven and the everlasting rest that awaits you there. Study the excellence and reality of your inheritance, and compare the joys of heaven with the passing pleasures of this world. Then pray that God would change your heart—from being in love with the world to being passionately in love with Him. Here are five reasons you can hope in your future heavenly rest.

1. You Can Hope in Heavenly Rest Because It Is True Rest. "Rest!" How sweet the sound. It is melody to my ears! It revives my heart like a cold glass of water and brings energy to my spirit—revitalizing my soul! Rest—not like a stone that rests lifelessly on the ground, nor like a corpse that rests in the grave. But an active rest—a true rest. It is a rest in which we "will not rest day and night, saying, 'Holy, holy, holy, Lord God Almighty!'" (See Revelation 4:8.) It is a rest in which we will rest from sin, but not from worship; from suffering and sorrow, but not from joy! What happiness that day will bring, when I will rest with God; when I will rest in knowing perfectly, loving completely, rejoicing endlessly, and praising eternally; when my perfect soul and my perfect body will be joined perfectly by God Himself; when God, who is love, will rest in His love to me as I will rest in my love to Him and rejoice in me as I will rejoice in Him. That is the essence of true rest, and it is the rest that every believer can look forward to in heaven.

2. You Can Hope in Heavenly Rest Because It Is Not Far Off. Christians tend to forget that their true rest is found in heaven. How quickly we complain when hardship and trials face us in this life. Yet, the day of rest is not far off. In fact, it is very near and coming soon. Christ is coming quickly and will not delay! Though the Lord seems to postpone His return, before long He will be here. What is a few hundred years when they are over? Especially compared to eternity! Certainly and suddenly He will appear, like lightning in the sky. At any moment we may hear the sound of the trumpet and see Him coming in the clouds with His angels. Even if He should wait a few more hundred years, we will go to Him in death. No matter the path, whether He comes to us or we go to Him, our eternal rest is fast approaching. Instead of complaining in this life, let's hold fast to the promises of the next.

3. You Can Hope in Heavenly Rest Because Christ Secured It for You. For Christians who have believed and obeyed, this eternal rest is part of the reward for their faith and patience. This is what we have prayed and waited for—many of us for an entire lifetime. Your fight against sin and temptation; your scars from the persecution of His enemies; your endurance in the midst of trials and affliction; this is the rest you have eagerly desired. This is the rest that Christ Himself secured for you through His death on the cross. Your heavenly crown was only made possible by His crown of thorns. Your heavenly mansion was purchased on a cross made of rough timber and crude nails. So, when you come into your heavenly rest, He will take you by the hand and lead you into His eternal kingdom, and your eternal home. The Father receives you as the bride of His Son and welcomes you to your glorious home. You are unworthy in and of yourself, yet you have been made worthy through the sacrifice of Christ. For that we will praise Him and give Him the glory forever!

4. You Can Hope in Heavenly Rest Because There Is No True Rest on Earth. In contrast to the true rest of heaven, there are many false rests on this earth, tempting us to turn to them for comfort rather than looking to Christ. Our hearts quickly turn to worldly delights and sinful pleasures in our search for satisfaction. But, is it better to be here than to be with God? Is the company better? Are the pleasures greater? Do not delay or make excuses; examine the Scriptures and see what heaven will be like. Remind yourself of the true wonders and delights of God's house. Resist looking back into the wilderness of sin, except to contrast it with the true joys of the kingdom where we will see the glorious New Jerusalem, the pearl-laden gates, the jewel-laden foundation, and the streets of gold. Even the sun that lights this world will be useless there, for the Father will be the sun and Christ will be the light. How sad it is that many in the world do not realize what they're missing. Instead of pursuing eternal rest and happiness, they settle for the passing pleasures of sin—pleasures that are nothing more than vanity.

5. You Can Hope in Heavenly Rest Because It Produces Eternal Joy and Praise. A God-promised rest! What joy that should produce, as no trial or temptation or anything on this earth can take it away from us. If we have given ourselves to Christ, He will bring us to the paradise of God; He will welcome us into the New Jerusalem; He will give us a taste of the Tree of Life. Even in waiting for that future reality, we rejoice in anticipation and in the hope of His glory. And our joy and praise will continue into eternity, for our rest will not be self-indulgent but will center on the worship of the Lamb for all eternity.

In the meantime, Christians have nothing to worry about. It was His work to purchase eternal life on our behalf—yours and mine; it is His to prepare a place for us, and to prepare us for it, and bring us to it. The eternal God of truth has given us His promise, His seal and oath, that, believing in Christ, we will not perish, but have everlasting life. So we will give praise to the One we trust and rejoice in our Redeemer. Nothing in the world can come close to evoking the same joy and happiness that the assurance of salvation brings. And this happiness will continue and increase when we come to heaven's gate. With a shout of joy we will enter the glorious heavenly temple, and with shouts of joy we will continue to worship Him forever.

LOOKING TOWARD THE FUTURE

Indeed, our future rest is one worth waiting for. We can eagerly anticipate it because we know that it is certain. We can cling to it when life gets hard. We can hold tightly to it when our faith is attacked. We can focus on it when we are tempted by the lie of worldly satisfaction. And we can strive to always be faithful as we pursue the things of heaven rather than the things of earth.

SEEING THE
DIFFERENCE

The Results of Hope in Everyday Life

CHAPTER 21

THE HAPPINESS HOPE BRINGS

Blessed [or happy] is he whose help is the God of Jacob,
whose hope is in the LORD his God.

PSALM 146:5

The pursuit of happiness—it has been one of the core values of American society ever since its inclusion as an unalienable right in the Declaration of Independence. It is what gets most people up in the morning, drags them to work, motivates them to work overtime, and encourages them to do it all over again. It is the basis for our capitalistic economy and the essence of the American Dream. It finances casinos and resorts, funds state lotteries, nourishes materialism, and sells romantic novels.

For most people, the pursuit of happiness is simply that, a pursuit. Happiness itself seems just out of reach. The new car, the new job, or the new outfit—they bring satisfaction for a little while, but then they get old and the search for happiness moves somewhere else. When hardship rolls in, like the storm clouds of winter, any lasting flicker of happiness fades into the darkness of depression and despair.

For Christians, however, God's Word goes one step further than the Declaration of Independence. Whereas even the best of human governments can only promise the pursuit of happiness, God promises His children that they can obtain happiness—if they look for it in Him.

In other words, by resting in His promises, they can find comfort even in the worst of circumstances; they can be glad in the hardest of trials; they can know peace even when the world around them is in turmoil. With this in mind, we will explore three ways in which hope brings lasting happiness.

1. Hope Brings Joy in the Midst of Trials. One of the greatest threats to happiness is that of hardship and tribulation. Life often brings us situations we don't understand, situations that seem unbearable, and times that are really tough. It might be a death in the family, a lack of funds, a personal health problem, or simply the pressures of a hectic schedule. Yet, even in the midst of these circumstances, hope allows us to find joy—here are three reasons why:

a. *Because trials force us to depend on God.* In Romans 5:3, Paul says that we should "rejoice in our sufferings, because we know that suffering produces perseverance." James echoes this in James 1:2–3 when he writes, "Consider it pure joy, my brothers, whenever you face trials of many kinds, because you know that the testing of your faith develops perseverance." In both of these passages, the point is clear: Hardship produces perseverance.

What is perseverance? Perseverance is the ability to wait on the Lord—the power to weather any storm because permanent shelter has been taken in God. You see, trials usually involve the loss of something we hold precious—whether it's our health, a family member, or our job. By taking away what we hold dear on this earth, trials force us to look to God; they force us to depend on Him. And rightly so, because only on the solid rock of His strength can we survive the storm—all other ground is sinking sand. Trials, then, teach us perseverance because they force us to wait on the Lord and rely on His power and His faithfulness (see Lamentations 3:20–25). In this way, they bring us into a closer communion with our heavenly Father. As His children, this deepened relationship brings great joy, even in the midst of great tragedy.

b. *Because trials are for our spiritual good.* Not only do trials produce perseverance, they also result in holiness in our lives. Romans 5:4 refers to this as proven character and James 1:4 as spiritual maturity. The author of Hebrews says this: "No discipline [trial] seems pleasant at the time, but painful. Later on, however, it produces a harvest of righteousness and peace for those who have been trained by it" (Hebrews 12:11). In other words, while life's hardships are never enjoyable, God always uses them for our benefit (Romans 8:28). Then we can rejoice, even in the worst of times, because we know that God is refining us in the process. We may not understand everything that is involved. We may not have all of our questions answered. But of this we can be sure: God loves His children more than we could ever know (1 John 4:11, 19). He wants us to be holy (1 Peter 1:15–16), and sometimes He uses trials to teach us things we would never have otherwise learned. Because we look forward to the sanctifying result in our lives, we can have joy despite the sorrow.

c. *Because trials cause us to long for heaven.* Not only do trials point us to a faithful God, they also remind us that earth is not our home—heaven is. In 2 Corinthians 4:17, Paul states, "For our light and momentary troubles are achieving for us an eternal glory that far outweighs them all." While he could have been focused on his earthly problems, Paul chose instead to look to his heavenly future. And it's not as though he was without hardship; he had experienced numerous difficulties—see 2 Corinthians 11:23–28 for a complete list. But Paul chose to rejoice in the reward that waited for him in the next life instead of focusing on his rough treatment here and now. We, too, have the biblical promise of a heavenly home—one in which our Savior will wipe every tear from our eyes (Revelation 21:4).

2. Hope Brings Contentment in the Midst of Materialism. A second threat to happiness, beyond trials, comes from the materialism of the world around us. Cleverly disguised as television commercials, magazine ads, and highway billboards, discontentment threatens to distract Christians with empty pursuits and temporary pleasures. Taking our eyes off of Christ, we think we can somehow find satisfaction in money and possessions. Yet, without fail, the things of this world never satisfy our hearts like we think they will; they never give us the happiness they promise. Hope, however, offers us true happiness, a happiness of which this world knows nothing—and it does so in at least two ways:

a. *By taking our eyes off of this world.* In combating discontentment, hope begins by taking our eyes off of the temporary and putting them on the eternal. In Hebrews 12:1–2, the author compares the Christian life to a race. In order to be faithful in the race, we must get rid of the sin in our lives, as well as any unhelpful distractions. Anything that might cause us to take our eyes off of our heavenly prize must be avoided—our focus cannot be both on earth and heaven at the same time.

Why would we want to get consumed by the things of earth anyway? Solomon, as we saw in chapter 12, tried everything he could to find satisfaction on this earth (Ecclesiastes 2). In the end, however, he realized that it is only found in God (Ecclesiastes 12:13–14). After all, the pursuits of this world are passing away (1 John 2:16–17; 2 Peter 3:10–12). Even Christ told His followers not to work overly hard to store up treasure on earth, when only the treasure of heaven lasts forever (Matthew 6:19–20). Because hope focuses us on God's promises for the future, it takes our eyes off of the false promises of this present world.

b. *By putting our eyes on the One who can satisfy.* In taking our eyes off of the things of earth, hope puts our eyes on the things of heaven. Or, more specifically, it puts our eyes on the Person of heaven, namely, Jesus Christ (see Hebrews 12:2). He is the only One who can truly satisfy us. He offers living water, such that those who drink never thirst again (John 4:13–14). He is the Bread of Life, such that those who eat never go hungry again (John 6:35). Simply said, He alone provides the spiritual nourishment that we all desire. In discussing all his religious achievements—which he once thought would satisfy him—Paul declares, "I consider everything a loss compared to the surpassing greatness of knowing Christ Jesus my Lord, for whose sake I have lost all things. I consider them rubbish, that I may gain Christ" (Philippians 3:8). Only God can fill the longings of our heart. So, hope looks to Him for satisfaction—and in so doing finds true happiness.

3. Hope Brings Peace in the Midst of Trouble. A third threat to happiness, in addition to trials and discontentment, is the temptation to worry. As we saw in chapter 11, worry is essentially emotional suffocation, with a potential problem becoming the focus of every thought. All that you do is affected. Life seems somehow a little darker, the shadows a little longer, and the air a little heavier. You have made a mountain out of what may not even become a molehill. But thankfully, the God of hope can help you stop worrying—giving you back the spiritual tranquility you've lost.

The apostle Paul had a lot of reasons to worry. The Jews wanted to kill him. The Gentiles thought he was crazy and a danger to society. And the churches he had planted were prone to division and false teaching. Yet, in situations where most of us would have complained, become worried, or grown discouraged, Paul reacted differently. In Philippians 4:6–7, he says this: "Do not be anxious about anything, but in everything, by prayer and petition, with thanksgiving, present your requests to God. And the peace of God, which transcends all understanding, will guard your hearts and your minds in Christ Jesus." In these two verses alone, Paul gives four means by which hope overcomes worry.

a. *Hope meets fear with faith.* From a human standpoint, Paul certainly had a lot to fear. Yet, in spite of his circumstances, he chose to put his hope in Christ. In fact, in Philippians 1:19–20, speaking specifically of his trying circumstances, Paul says, "I know that through your prayers and the help given by the Spirit of Jesus Christ, what has happened to me will turn out for my deliverance. I eagerly expect and hope that I will in no way be ashamed, but will have sufficient courage so that now as always Christ will be exalted in my body, whether by life or by death." Because his hope was in Christ, he chose to cling by faith to God's promises rather than worry about anything. As Christians, we, too, can hope in God rather than our circumstances. After all, the God we serve is bigger than any fear we might have. As Paul commands his readers, "Be anxious for nothing" (Philippians 4:6 NKJV).

b. *Hope meets worry with worship.* Paul continues by telling the Philippians that they should respond to "everything" in life "with thanksgiving." Instead of worrying about the details of what may or may not happen, believers are to praise God for His faithfulness in their lives. In Philippians 4:8, Paul implores Christians to think about things that are true, right, and noble. When we worry, our minds concentrate on things that are harmful and will probably never happen. In contrast, we should be meditating on those things that we know are certain—such as God's power, goodness, and trustworthiness. God's promises, rather than the potential troubles of the future, should govern our lives.

c. *Hope meets problems with prayer.* Rather than worrying about our problems, Paul commands us to take them to the Lord "by prayer and petition." In 1 Thessalonians 5:17, he echoes this by telling us to "pray continually." Often, Christians find unceasing prayer hard to practice. Yet, when we worry, we find it easy to worry continually. Instead, we should turn our worries into prayer requests. In so doing, we will learn to depend on the Lord—trusting in Him rather than in our own strength.

d. *Hope replaces pressure with peace.* In Philippians 4:7, Paul concludes by assuring his readers that when they rest in God, His peace will comfort them. Instead of being consumed by worry, we can find peace when we choose to rely on God. Worry, of course, never brings happiness—it brings agitation, stress, and tension. God, on the other hand, promises internal peace to those who hope in Him. This type of peace can never be disrupted by external circumstances. No matter what happens, the hopeful believer can always be happy—by relying on the God of hope.

HAPPY ARE THE HOPEFUL

Hope won't necessarily change your situation. Even the most hopeful person will experience times of difficulty, sadness, and loss. Yet, when we focus on God's promises rather than our problems, we can find true joy, contentment, and peace no matter what life brings our way.

Sadly, the happiness of the worldly is based on circumstances. If things are going well, happiness comes easy. When things are not going well, happiness is nowhere to be found. In contrast, the happiness of hope is based on certainty. God has made certain promises, and those promises do not change no matter what happens in this life. So, while the world's happiness is only temporary—making it nothing more than a continual pursuit—the happiness God offers lasts for-ever, even in the midst of sorrow and tragedy. As His children, may we cling to the promises of His Word and find our joy in Him.

CHAPTER 22

THE COMFORT HOPE PROVIDES

May our Lord Jesus Christ himself and God our Father,
who loved us and by his grace gave us eternal encouragement and good hope,
encourage your hearts and strengthen you in every good deed and word.

2 THESSALONIANS 2:16–17

Emotional hurt is always far more painful than physical affliction—to be betrayed, abandoned, or despised by someone you love; to experience the loss of a family member or friend; to be wrongly attacked or criticized by those around you. Certainly, physical hardship is painful—whether the trial involves your finances, your job, your health, or your possessions. Yet, emotional suffering cuts deeper, starting on the inside and working its way out.

Jesus Himself, having been beaten and scourged by the Roman guards, felt His greatest agony not when He was nailed to the cross, but rather when He cried out, "My God, my God, why have you forsaken me?" (Matthew 27:46). For Jacob, the pain came when he thought Joseph was dead (Genesis 37:34–35). David felt it through the betrayal and death of his son Absalom (2 Samuel 15–19). And for

Jeremiah, it came when his beloved city of Jerusalem was destroyed (Lamentations 3:20–25). Even Job's sufferings included the loss of all his children and the bad advice of his closest friends (see Job 2).

Deep emotional pain also found its way into the apostle Paul's life. When it came to physical pain, Paul counted his trials as joy (2 Corinthians 7:4). In 2 Corinthians 11:24–27, he tells about his troubles—including being beaten, stoned, shipwrecked, and constantly on the move. Yet, these trials paled in comparison to the emotional hardships that he faced. In fact, it was his daily "concern for all the churches" that occupied his mind more than any of his physical torments (v. 28). Nevertheless, because of the hope he had in God, Paul was able to respond rightly to even life's hardest situations. Consequently, he found comfort in situations where comfort is not easily found.

PAUL EXPERIENCED ALL TYPES OF EMOTIONAL PAIN

Paul, it seems, felt nearly every type of emotional pain. In fact, it all came to a head at the end of his life, while he was in prison awaiting execution. In 2 Timothy 4:9–16 Paul describes this pain for us—pain that came in five different ways.

1. Paul experienced the pain of betrayal (2 Timothy 4:9–10). In verse 10, Paul tells Timothy that Demas had betrayed him. Instead of continuing in the faith, Demas left Paul for the pursuits of this world. He denied the faith and walked away—not because of anything Paul had done, but rather because Demas "loved this world."

From other places in Scripture we find that Demas was one of Paul's closest friends. In Colossians 4:14, he is mentioned along with Luke as one of Paul's traveling companions. In Philemon 24 he is listed as one of Paul's "fellow workers." He was not just an acquaintance or a casual friend. No, he was one of Paul's trusted associates, a close companion, and a beloved comrade. But, when he was most needed, he deserted Paul, forsaking the apostle and his teaching for the passing pleasures of sin.

How this must have haunted Paul. He must have wondered why he didn't see it coming. Could he have prevented it? Was he somehow responsible? How could his friend have turned on him? Needless to say, Paul knew what it was to be betrayed.

2. Paul experienced the pain of loneliness (2 Timothy 4:10–13). Along with betrayal, Paul felt the pain of loneliness. At the end of verse 10, he notes that not only has Demas left, but both Crescens and Titus are gone, too. While Crescens and Titus appear to have left on good terms and for ministerial reasons, Paul nonetheless feels the pain of loneliness. This is heightened by the fact that he sent Tychicus to Ephesus (v. 12). Thankfully, Luke is still with him (v. 11). Yet, he misses his friends who are not there. So, he urges Timothy to come quickly and to bring Mark along, too (v. 11). At the end of his life, Paul longed for the fellowship of his friends. Nevertheless, at least for the moment, he endured the pain of loneliness.

3. Paul experienced the pain of adversity (2 Timothy 4:14–15). Paul also experienced pain through the presence of his enemies. In verses 14–15, he tells Timothy about Alexander the metalworker, a man who is causing him great harm—presumably by verbally assaulting both Paul's reputation and the message he proclaimed. Although we don't know for sure, Alexander was possibly an idol maker (like the idol makers of Acts 19:24–26) who wanted Paul silenced because the gospel was hurting his business. Whatever the case, he was greatly opposing Paul—and Paul felt the pain of his attack.

4. Paul experienced the pain of abandonment (2 Timothy 4:16). Paul's emotional pain continued with the pain of abandonment. In verse 16 he says this: "At my first defense, no one came to my support, but everyone deserted me. May it not be held against them." Here Paul was, on trial for his life, and no one was there to support him. Where was Luke or anyone else? Paul doesn't tell us. Yet, it seems clear that at his most vulnerable point in life, his friends had all abandoned him. Whether they had good excuses or not is beside the point. The fact remains—Paul felt the pain of abandonment because no one supported him when he needed them the most.

5. Paul experienced the pain of false accusation (2 Timothy 4:16). Along with everything else, Paul endured the pain of false accusation. We know from church history that he died shortly after this letter was written. As had been the case at his other trials (Acts 25–26), angry Jewish leaders—perhaps led by Alexander the metalworker—falsely charged Paul with being a heretical insurrectionist. Nero, apparently swayed by their arguments, eventually gave the command for Paul to be executed. Paul did not die because he was a criminal, but because he was a faithful Christian who was wrongfully accused. Paul knew what it was to be unjustly condemned.

PAUL'S RESPONSE TO EMOTIONAL PAIN

So how did Paul deal with these emotional tragedies? Did he give up? Did he fall into a deep depression or contemplate suicide? No. Instead, he chose to lean upon God's promises rather than his failing circumstances. His friends may not have been there for him, but God would never leave his side. In fact, in 2 Timothy 4:17–18, Paul explains the four things he did to deal with the emotional pain in his life. As a result, he remained hopeful by finding comfort in God.

1. Paul found his strength in Christ (2 Timothy 4:17). While his pain was certainly very deep and very real, Paul chose to focus on his Savior rather than his circumstances. In light of this, in verse 17, he remarks that although his friends were nowhere to be found, "the Lord stood at my side and gave me strength." His attitude is that of Moses and the Israelites, who, after being rescued from the pursuing

Egyptians, sing, "The LORD is my strength and my song; he has become my salvation. He is my God, and I will praise him, my father's God, and I will exalt him" (Exodus 15:2). His attitude is that of David, who exclaims, "The LORD is my strength and my shield; my heart trusts in him, and I am helped. My heart leaps for joy and I will give thanks to him in song" (Psalm 28:7). His attitude is that of Jews in Isaiah 12:2, who one day will shout, "Surely God is my salvation; I will trust and not be afraid. The LORD, the LORD, is my strength and my song; he has become my salvation." Like Paul, our response to pain should be dependence on the strength which God alone supplies, knowing that through Him any situation can be endured (Philippians 4:13).

2. **Paul remained faithful in his ministry (2 Timothy 4:17).** Not only did Paul rely on God's strength rather than his own, he remained faithful to the ministry God had given him. In fact, at the end of verse 17, Paul says that through the Lord's power he was able to faithfully proclaim the gospel message to the Gentiles who were there. Paul could have kept silent. He could have watered down the truth. After all, he was on trial for his life. Besides, none of his friends were there— so no one would have known if he had compromised just once. But, instead of using his situation as an excuse, Paul remained faithful because he feared God more than he feared men.

What a contrast this is to many in our churches today. When times get tough, it's easy to tap out of ministry for awhile. Maybe the pain is so great, we don't feel like going to church for a time. Maybe the hurt is so deep, we don't want to reach out and care for others. Instead, we wallow in self-pity and bitter pride. But this is not the right response. Paul never used his personal pain as an excuse for unfaithfulness, and neither should we.

3. **Paul looked forward to heaven (2 Timothy 4:18).** Not only did Paul rely on God's strength to continue in his ministry, he eagerly looked forward to heaven. In the first half of verse 18, he writes,

"The Lord will rescue me from every evil attack and will bring me safely to his heavenly kingdom." Notice Paul's confidence in his Savior. There is no doubting that God will rescue him. Notice, as well, that Paul doesn't equate this rescue with being set free. He knows that he will probably die (see v. 6). Nevertheless, for Paul the rescue was much, much greater. It was a rescue from all of the pain and hardship of this world—a rescue into the heavenly kingdom of God. By keeping his eyes on heaven, Paul was able to find joy even during life's hardships—simply by remembering that nothing in this life could keep him from the glorious future God had promised.

4. Paul gave God the glory (2 Timothy 4:18). Finally, despite his hardship, Paul continued to worship God and give Him praise. At the end of verse 18, he exclaims: "To him be glory for ever and ever. Amen." Paul was facing execution; he had been betrayed, deserted, attacked, abandoned, and falsely accused. Yet, he still gave God the glory. Why? Because God never left his side. Ever since Paul's conversion on the Damascus road (Acts 9:1–19), Jesus Christ had never forsaken him. Throughout his life, his Lord and Savior had always been faithful. Even in his final days, when he felt isolated from his human associates, Paul knew he could still rely on his all-powerful God. Instead of crying out in blasphemous anger or floundering in self-pity, Paul chose to praise the Savior he trusted. After all, the apostle understood that God was in control and that He knew what He was doing.

FINDING OUR COMFORT IN CHRIST

When emotional pain stabs our hearts, we, like Paul, should respond by leaning on Christ, being faithful in our ministry, looking forward to heaven, and giving glory to God. Of course, we can only do this if we trust His promises, namely, that He will never leave us or forsake us (Hebrews 13:5), that He will reward us for our faithfulness (Matthew 16:27), that He is preparing a place for us (John 14:2), and that He is working all things for our good (Romans 8:28).

Robert Louis Stevenson tells a story about a ship in the midst of a storm, heading desperately near the rocky shore. The vessel's passengers were all huddled below in worry. In desperation, one of them ran up to the deck despite the danger of being washed overboard. There at the wheel he saw the ship's pilot, steadily inching the wheel to turn the ship back toward the sea. In the midst of the chaos, the pilot glanced back, saw the onlooker, and smiled. The passenger then went back down to the others and, with a note of cheer, exclaimed: "I have seen the face of the pilot and he smiled. All is well."

As believers, Jesus Christ is our pilot. The storm may be great, but He's still at the wheel, directing the ship to safety. Let us look to Him when emotional hardship comes—for in seeing His smile we will be certain that all is well.

CHAPTER 23

THE COURAGE HOPE IGNITES

Therefore, since we have such a hope, we are very bold.

2 CORINTHIANS 3:12

The year was A.D. 162. Bishop Polycarp of Smyrna was on the Roman government's "most wanted list." His crime was being a Christian. When he was found, he fed dinner to the Roman guards who had come to arrest him. He then asked for an hour in prayer, which they permitted him to have. Yet his prayer was so fervent and passionate that his captors regretted even being involved in his apprehension.

Appearing before a Roman proconsul, Polycarp stood firm. The proconsul even urged him to deny Christ, "Swear, and I will release you—reproach Christ." But Polycarp's faith was undeterred: "Eighty and six years have I served Him, and He never once wronged me; how then shall I blaspheme my King, who has saved me?" When it was clear that Polycarp would not recant, he was sentenced to be burned at the stake.

In being executed, however, Polycarp was only tied to the stake rather than nailed to it as was customary, because he assured his executioners that he would not move. And he did not move, but rather died courageously for the Lord whom he loved.

The year was A.D. 249 when Chrysostom was captured for being a Christian. He was tied inside a leather bag full of snakes and scorpions. The bag was then thrown into the sea.

The year was A.D. 287 when Acquitain, a Christian woman from France, was broiled on a gridiron because of her faith. Her burned body was then beheaded.

The year was A.D. 308 when Quirinus, the bishop of Siscia, was taken before the governor and commanded to sacrifice to pagan deities. When he refused, he was sent to prison in order that the tortures of jail might persuade him to reconsider. Somehow prison only reinforced Quirinus's resolve. So the governor put him in chains and led him through the surrounding towns and villages, exposing him to ridicule wherever he went. When he still would not recant, he was sentenced to drown with a stone fastened around his neck.

The year was A.D. 1414 when John Huss was arrested for preaching the truth of the gospel as had his mentor John Wycliffe. He was condemned and sentenced to burn at the stake. When the chain was put around him at the stake, he said with a smile, "My Lord Jesus Christ was bound with a harder chain than this for my sake, and why then should I be ashamed of this rusty one?" And when asked to abjure, he declined saying, "What I taught with my lips I now seal with my blood." As the flames engulfed his body, John Huss died singing a hymn.

The year was A.D. 2002 when Kungri Masih, a Christian man in Pakistan, was sentenced to death for violating Pakistan's "blasphemy law." Just fourteen months earlier, a twenty-three-year-old Pakistani Bible college student, named Sheraz, was found dead outside his church. A note on his body said, "Stop preaching to Muslims."

These examples could be multiplied almost without number. Yet the essence of all these stories is the same. Ordinary people saved by God were transformed into courageous heroes because of their hope. Nothing, not even death itself, could cause them to doubt the promises of God. They paid the ultimate price—choosing to embrace the glories of heaven rather than the approval of men.

Put yourself in their shoes for a moment. Imagine that the police broke into your house one night and dragged you away from your family. Imagine that the next day you stood trial before an unjust tribunal. Imagine that they gave you only one choice—deny Jesus Christ or be executed immediately. Which would you choose? Why would you make that choice? And how would knowing that God's promises are true influence your decision?

By God's grace, most Christians in North America and other western countries have never had to undergo this type of traumatic experience. Yet, every day we are faced with other opportunities to show courage by taking a stand for Christ. Maybe it's an evangelistic opportunity with a coworker; maybe it involves not participating in shady business practices with an overeager partner; maybe it's something as simple as telling the truth when everyone else is asking you to lie. Whatever the situation, Scripture commands us to courageously do what we know to be right, standing firm for the faith we profess, and willingly enduring the consequences. In light of this, biblical hope provides us with three motivations for true courage.

1. Hope Ignites Courage Because the Future Is Secure. First, hope motivates courage by reminding us that the future is certain. While the fears of the present may seem overwhelming, the facts of the future far outmatch them. We may be mocked by our peers for sharing the gospel, but one day we will be in heaven with our Savior. We may lose our job for taking a stand for the truth, but one day we will be rewarded by Christ. We may be distanced from our closest friends or even our family, but one day we will spend eternity with our loving Father. We may even be killed, but one day we will be raised again when Jesus returns.

The apostle Paul had this same attitude when he was in prison awaiting trial. Not knowing whether he would be freed or killed, Paul's concern was simply that he would proclaim his Christian faith courageously (Ephesians 6:19–20). He could take this stand because he wasn't concerned with the immediate outcome—the verdict of his trial. What mattered to him was that his heavenly Master be honored. In fact, in Philippians 1:20 he writes, "I eagerly expect and hope that I will in no way be ashamed, but will have sufficient courage so that now as always Christ will be exalted in my body, whether by life or by death."

As we've seen in previous chapters, our heavenly hope is overflowing—we have the promise of eternal rest, the promise of eternal reward, the promise of eternal bliss, and the promise of eternal life. When we act on these God-given guarantees, there is nothing on this earth that can intimidate us. Our God is bigger than any human threat; He has conquered death itself (2 Timothy 1:10); He has promised us an everlasting home in heaven; our job is simply to be faithful and let Him take care of the details.

2. Hope Ignites Courage Because God Is in Control. God has not only secured our future, but He is also in complete control of the present. He is the sovereign King of the universe (Psalm 115:3), and there is nothing that can happen without either His stipulation or permission. Even the persecution of His own saints is something He allows. Job is an example of this—a faithful man who endured great trials all within parameters that God had set (see Job 1–2).

In Daniel 3, Shadrach, Meshach, and Abednego (three of Daniel's friends) courageously refused to worship Nebuchadnezzar's golden image (vv. 1–12). When the king learned of their actions, he was furious and demanded that they either worship the idol or be burned alive. Unwavering, the three men chose the second option (see vv. 16–18). As a result of their conviction, they were bound and thrown into Nebuchadnezzar's fiery furnace.

Of course, it is true that in this case God miraculously saved His faithful servants. Shadrach, Meshach, and Abednego were untouched by the flames (Daniel 3:26–27). Nevertheless, these men did not know the outcome of their choice until after they had already made it. What they did know, however, was that their God, the true God, was in control. They chose to stay faithful and to trust Him with the end results. Their courage came from their confidence in God.

3. Hope Ignites Courage Because Our Treasure Is in Heaven. Because Christ has promised us a future reward, our treasure truly is in heaven rather than on this earth (Matthew 6:19–20). This means there is nothing in this world of more value or worth than the inheritance we have in heaven.

Understanding this promotes courage because it forces us to realize that, no matter how the world threatens us, we ultimately have nothing to lose. If they threaten to persecute us, we can rejoice because we have heavenly reward (Acts 5:41). If they threaten to kill us, we can rejoice because our eternity is certain. If they threaten to take away our homes, our possessions, our jobs, or even our families—we will still stand firm because our hope is not ultimately in any of those things. After all, the Lord Himself says, "If anyone comes to me and does not hate his father and mother, his wife and children, his brothers and sisters—yes, even his own life—he cannot be my disciple," (Luke 14:26). In saying this, Jesus simply means that our love for Him must be so strong that we would be willing to give up any other relationship for His sake.

The Lord even promises to reward our courage. In Matthew 5:11–12, He says, "Blessed are you when people insult you, persecute you and falsely say all kinds of evil against you because of me. Rejoice and be glad, because great is your reward in heaven, for in the same way they persecuted the prophets who were before you." With this in mind, we can be encouraged to know that, in expecting us to be faithful no matter what the cost, God will always be gracious to reward our perseverance.

When we stand courageously for what we believe, we prove that our hope is based in heaven—because what we truly value is stored there. On the other hand, when we give in to peer pressure or fear, we betray the fact that our hope, at least at that moment, has been placed in the things of this world. Put another way, we show that we value this life more than we value the next, that we value human acceptance more than the Lord's approval, and that we value earthly riches more than heavenly treasure. By contrast, true courage looks to the promises of God, in faith, and acts accordingly. In sum, hope in God's promises fills people with courage, while hope in this world fills people with cowardice.

REIGNITING YOUR COURAGE

As members of God's family, we can show courage even in the midst of persecution and pending death (Hebrews 3:6). After all, the Lord Himself is our confidence (Psalms 31:24, 71:5). He is our Strength and our Defense (Psalm 28:8). As Romans 8:31 asks, "If God is for us, who can be against us?"

God's Word gives many examples of men and women who were courageous because they held on to God's promises rather than looking at their own circumstances. Daniel's three friends provide one of these examples. Paul provides another—having been imprisoned and ultimately killed for the hope that he possessed (see Acts 26:7–8, 28:20). Hebrews 11 includes many more examples, as does the record of church history throughout the last two thousand years. Even Peter, who denied Christ at one point in his life (Matthew 26:69–75), later stood courageously before the Jewish leaders who had crucified Jesus (Acts 4:1–12). In 1 Peter 3:15, he gives this admonition: "But in your hearts set apart Christ as Lord. Always be prepared to give an answer to everyone who asks you to give the reason for the hope that you have."

By looking to God's Word and His promises, and by trusting those promises, every Christian can find courage in any situation. After all, courage is really a matter of trust—trusting your heavenly Father rather than your human-induced fear. Author Jerry Bridges says this:

> *Trusting God is a matter of faith, and faith is the fruit of the Spirit (Galatians 5:22). Only the Holy Spirit can make His Word come alive in our hearts and create faith, but we can choose to look to Him to do that, or we can choose to be ruled by our feelings of anxiety or resentment or grief.*[1]

So the question is, will we be ruled by fear or ruled by faith? Will we look to the promises of earth or the promises of heaven? Will we be conquerors or cowards? (See Revelation 2:7, 11, 17, 26–28; 3:5, 12, 21.) When we hope in God, we can be confident that we will answer these questions correctly and in so doing find the key to courage.

CHAPTER 24

THE HOLINESS HOPE MOTIVATES

Everyone who has this hope in him purifies himself, just as he [Christ] is pure.

1 JOHN 3:3

As we go about the business of our daily lives, we would do well to pay attention to the words written by Robert Murray McCheyne to his friend Dan Edwards on October 2, 1840. Edwards had recently been sent to Germany as a missionary.

> *I know you will apply hard to [learn] German; but do not forget the culture of the inner man—I mean of the heart. . . . In great measure, according to the purity and perfections of the instrument, will be the success. It is not great talents God blesses so much as likeness to Jesus. A holy minister is an awful [powerful] weapon in the hand of God.[1]*

Said another way, personal holiness matters. Obedience and faithfulness to His Word—these are the means by which God measures success. And lest someone think this only applies to missionaries, listen to the words of J. C. Ryle:

> *Whatever we may think fit to say, we must be holy, if we would see the Lord. Where is our Christianity if we are not? We must not merely have a Christian name, and Christian knowledge, we must have a Christian character also. We must be saints on earth, if ever we mean to be saints in heaven. God has said it, and He will not go back: "Without holiness no man shall see the Lord."*[2]

Clearly, then, every believer is commanded to "be holy, because I [God] am holy" (1 Peter 1:16). There is no excuse for laziness, no room for self-indulgence, and no place for pride. We are to put off our old way of thinking and replace it with right thinking (Ephesians 4:22–24; Philippians 4:8). We are to deny sinful deeds and replace them with the fruit of the Spirit (Galatians 5:19–24). We are to put to death our wickedness (Colossians 3:5) by the power of the Spirit (Romans 8:13). Of course, we will never be totally sinless until we reach heaven (1 John 1:8–10). Nevertheless, we chase after righteousness (2 Timothy 2:22) knowing that "The LORD detests the way of the wicked but he loves those who pursue righteousness" (Proverbs 15:9). Practically speaking, holiness manifests itself in our lives through genuine obedience to God's commands. Even the term "holiness," referring to "separation," points to this idea—we are to separate ourselves from the sinful activities of this world in order to be more fully devoted to God.

Granted, the pursuit of holiness in our lives is not easy (see Romans 7:15–24). Yet, God is faithful, not only to forgive, but also to sanctify and purify the lives of those whom He has saved. The wonderful reality, then, is that although the process of our sanctification takes discipline and hard work, God ultimately gives us both the power and the victory (see 1 Thessalonians 5:23–24).

Not only is God our source of strength in the midst of temptation, He also gives us great motivation to obey—motivation that is intrinsically tied to our hope. In other words, His promises to us are coupled with His expectations for us. Here are three reasons that our hope should motivate our daily obedience.

1. Hope Motivates Obedience Because the Master Is Returning. Knowing that the Lord could return at any moment should be a great motivation for continued faithfulness. In Revelation 22:12, Jesus says, "Behold, I am coming soon! My reward is with me, and I will give to everyone according to what he has done." Should we not earnestly desire to be pleasing to Him when He comes? Of course, this does not mean that our salvation is based on our works (see Ephesians 2:8–10). Our salvation is God's free gift of grace, bestowed on all who genuinely repent and believe (Romans 10:9–10). At the same time, however, we are rewarded in accordance with our obedience. Romans 14:10 simply states that "we will all stand before God's judgment seat." Just as an exceptional employee receives a bonus or an outstanding soldier a decorative medal, Christ's loyal servants will be rewarded according to their deeds.

Of course, God is not impressed with the mere outward appearance of righteousness. He does not reward actions or words that come from a hard, selfish heart. Our God knows the thoughts of men (Jeremiah 17:9–10). He is well aware of our motives (Proverbs 16:2). So, unless our works stem from a genuine desire to please Him, there is no reward. After all, the Pharisees did good works. But since they did them with wrong motives, they did not receive our Lord's approval (Matthew 6:1–6).

Hope-motivated holiness, then, stems from a genuine desire to love the Lord and keep His commands (Mark 12:30; John 14:15). Even if no one sees or knows, God sees and God knows—the motivation is not human recognition, but rather heavenly reward. Having been saved by grace through faith, we work hard to be found faithful as His servants (Matthew 25:21), knowing that our greatest aim and highest satisfaction is found in pleasing Him (Colossians 1:10).

2. Hope Motivates Holiness Because God's Promises Can Be Believed. Second, hope motivates holiness because hope believes the promises of God over the promises of sin. In fact, temptation— which is where sin always begins (James 1:13–15)—is nothing more than a promise (albeit a false promise), claiming that true happiness is actually found in disobedience. Satan used this very tactic in the Garden of Eden when he promised Eve that, by disobeying God, she and Adam would be like God Himself (Genesis 3:5). Of course, the promise was a lie, but Eve chose to believe it anyway.

On the flip side, God also makes us promises. He promises that He knows what is best for us. He promises that He loves us as His children. He promises that He alone can satisfy. He promises that sin has terrible consequences. He promises that He will bless obedience. As one writer puts it, "Faith [and hope] and holiness are inextricably linked. Obeying the commands of God usually involves believing the promises of God."[3]

So, when temptation comes, the Christian has a choice. Faced with two sets of promises, the believer must decide which promises to believe. Both sides promise happiness and fulfillment. Both promise to have your best interests in mind. And yet, as we know from both Scripture and experience, the promises of sin are always false; they always let us down; they always disappoint; and they always lead to negative consequences. The promises of God, however, are always true; they never let us down; they never disappoint; and they always result in eternal reward. When we choose to believe God's promises consistently, holiness is the natural result.

For example, the pride of life (1 John 2:16) can be combated by God's promises—namely, His promise that those who are "poor in spirit" and "meek" will be "blessed" (Matthew 5:3–5), finding salvation (Psalm 149:4) and grace (Proverbs 3:34), and being lifted up in due time (James 4:10; 1 Peter 5:6). On the other hand, those who are proud will be brought low (Psalm 18:27; Job 40:12) and destroyed (Proverbs 15:25; Isaiah 2:17).

The lusts of the flesh (1 John 2:16)—including sexual sins, laziness, self-indulgence, and drunkenness—can also be combated by God's promises. Regarding sexual temptation and sensuality, God promises that sex will only bring true joy when it is enjoyed in its proper context—within the marriage relationship (1 Corinthians 7:2, 9–10; Hebrews 13:4). Regarding laziness, God says that "the sluggard craves and gets nothing, but the desires of the diligent are fully satisfied" (Proverbs 13:4). In response to self-indulgence, God promises that "it is more blessed to give than to receive" (Acts 20:35; Philippians 2:1–4). And in response to drunkenness, God promises that alcoholism will only lead to poor decisions and a wasted life (Proverbs 20:1). Again, the bottom line is that God alone can satisfy and bring lasting happiness. When we look for our fulfillment anyplace other than Him, we replace the spring of living water—that continually satisfies—with broken cisterns that are all dried up (Jeremiah 2:13).

The lusts of the eyes (1 John 2:16) can likewise be combated by God's promises. Covetousness, greed, and envy cannot make you happy, says God. Instead, contentment in His plan, His timing, and His wisdom are what bring lasting peace (Philippians 4:6). Scripture even says that we can look to Christ as the source of our contentment (Philippians 4:12–13). Wanting what others have will never bring true satisfaction, because human nature will always want more (Proverbs 27:20), but "godliness with contentment is great gain" (1 Timothy 6:6). Being thankful for what God has given you, and looking to Him for your fulfillment—this is where true satisfaction is found. After all, He promises to provide you with everything you need (Matthew 6:25–34; Philippians 4:19).

Sin takes place, then, when we doubt the promises of God and, instead, choose to believe the promises of our wicked flesh. As Christians, we must use "the sword of the Spirit, which is the word of God" (Ephesians 6:17) and counteract the lies of sin with the truth of Scripture. In so doing, we will choose the way of life rather than the way of death (Psalm 119:9–11).

3. Hope Motivates Holiness Because Divine Encouragement Is Promised. God certainly gives us incentives to obey—offering us both an eternal reward and the true promises of His Word. He also encourages us along the way, forgiving us when we fail and strengthening us when we are weak.

God heartens our daily walk in several ways. First, He promises us that, as believers, our future is secure. With this in mind, after discussing his own struggles, Paul can joyfully announce, "Therefore, there is now no condemnation for those who are in Christ Jesus" (Romans 8:1). We can be encouraged to keep fighting because we know that once we are part of His family, we will never be disowned. There is nothing, not even our own sin, that can separate us from the love of God in Christ Jesus (Romans 8:38–39).

Second, God cheers our hearts by reminding us that our struggle here is only temporary. One day, our battles with sin will be no more; our past failures will be history; our wrong choices will no longer be an issue. The resurrection body God creates for us will have no sinful remnant, nor will our heavenly home have any external solicitations to sin. We will be perfect forever.

Finally, God comforts us by promising that the process He started when He called us to Himself, He will ultimately finish. While this does not excuse laziness on our part, it does mean that we can depend on Him as we strive to be holy. After all, what Paul told the Thessalonian believers is true for all Christians—namely, that "from the beginning God chose you to be saved through the sanctifying work of the Spirit and through belief in the truth" (2 Thessalonians 2:13; see also 1 Peter 1:2). By relying on His Spirit, His strength, and His Word, we can be confident that we will find victory as we diligently pursue Him each day.

THE KEY TO HOLY LIVING

As we have seen, holiness is what God requires of His people. In fact, the Bible teaches that you can identify a true believer by looking at his behavior patterns—by looking to see whether his life is characterized by holy living (Matthew 7:18–20; Romans 8:5–14). But, bottom line, what is the key to holy living? John Piper answers that question like this, "The key to purity and holiness, the key to lasting effectiveness in all of life [is] constant contemplation on the glory of Christ."[4]

In other words, our relationship with and love for Christ must be the fuel that powers our holy living and obedience. Hope is an intrinsic part of this equation. Because when we look to our heavenly reward, we are looking ultimately to pleasing and glorifying Christ. When we choose to believe the promises of God rather than the promises of sin, we are choosing to trust in Christ and His Word—recognizing that Jesus alone can truly satisfy us. And when we look to His promises to encourage us along the way, we are relying not on ourselves but rather on Him.

As we run through this life, "let us throw off everything that hinders and the sin that so easily entangles, and. . .fix our eyes on Jesus, the author and perfecter of our faith" (Hebrews 12:1–2). After all, our only hope for holiness is in putting our hope in Him.

CHAPTER 25

THE FAITH HOPE INSTILLS

Now faith is being sure of what we hope for
and certain of what we do not see.

HEBREWS 11:1

What is faith? Webster defines it as "the assent of the mind to the truth of what is declared by another, resting on his authority and veracity, without other evidence."[1] For the Christian then, faith is believing that the promises of God are true simply because He says they are true. So when "hope" is used as a verb, hope and faith are virtually synonymous.

As a noun, hope refers directly to the promises of God. In this vein, the author of Hebrews, in Hebrews 6:17–19, writes:

> *Because God wanted to make the unchanging nature of his purpose very clear to the heirs of what was promised, he confirmed it with an oath. God did this so that, by two unchangeable things in which it is impossible for God to lie, we who have fled to take hold of the*

hope offered to us may be greatly encouraged. We have
this hope as an anchor for the soul, firm and secure.

But as a verb, hope speaks of our response to God's promises. In other words, because He offers us hope (noun form), we can hope (verb form) in Him and His guarantees. Or, put another way, we can have faith in His promises, meaning that we can believe them with confidence.

Scripture is clear that God is entirely trustworthy. Titus 1:2 (NKJV) even says that "God...cannot lie." As His children, we should live in faith, letting the reality of God's promises, even when we can't see them yet, govern our actions. Those who live in doubt—the opposite of faith—are essentially denying that the hope God gives is actually true. Charles Spurgeon said it like this:

> *I would recommend you either believe God up to the*
> *hilt, or else not to believe at all. Believe this book of God,*
> *every letter of it, or else reject it. There is no logical*
> *standing place between the two. Be satisfied with noth-*
> *ing less than a faith that swims in the deeps of divine*
> *revelation; a faith that paddles about the edge of the*
> *water is poor faith at best. It is little better than a dry-*
> *land faith, and is not good for much.*[2]

Certainly it's not always easy to trust God. Doubt, despair, and fear continually work their way into our lives—sometimes through our own personal trials, sometimes from the hypocrisy we see in other Christians, and sometimes through the attacks of non-Christian critics. Small questions have a way of sprouting into looming uncertainties, and suddenly our minds reel with skepticism and disbelief. Even Jesus' disciples were constantly being rebuked for having too little faith (Matthew 6:30, 8:26, 14:31, 16:8, 17:20).

Yet, it is when our faith is stretched that we need, most desperately, to remind ourselves of the promises of God. In remembering His gracious guarantees—as given in His Word—we can overcome our anxiety, doubt, and gloom. After all, the God we serve is bigger than any problem we face.

John Bunyan (1628–1688) was a man who understood this very thing. Because he would not stop preaching, he was thrown in prison. In fact, it was while incarcerated (during his second imprisonment), that he penned his best-known volume *The Pilgrim's Progress*—a book about which *Foxe's Book of Martyrs* says, "There is no doubt but that *The Pilgrim's Progress* has been more helpful than any other book but the Bible."

Written as an allegorical account of the life of a believer named "Christian," it uses simple narrative to convey deep spiritual truth. Christian, who is on his way to the Celestial City (or heaven), is traveling along the King's highway with his friend Hopeful. Together, they encounter many dangers and, by God's grace, they survive them all. One such peril comes from Doubting Castle—a terrible fortress of fear owned by Giant Despair. Symbolizing the doubts and fear that many believers face, Doubting Castle is finally overcome when Christian and Hopeful rely on the promise of God. This masterful story goes like this:[3]

A TRIP TO DOUBTING CASTLE

After a hard night's journey, Christian and Hopeful finally fell asleep. But, little did they know, the place where they slept was only a short distance from Doubting Castle, the owner of which was Giant Despair. In fact, they were actually sleeping on his property.

Early that next morning, when Giant Despair awoke and took a walk through his fields, he caught Christian and Hopeful asleep on his grounds. So, with a grim and surly voice, he woke them up and demanded to know why they were there.

Startled by their abrupt arousal, they quickly explained to him that they were pilgrims, and that they had lost their way. In response, the giant bellowed, "Because you have trespassed onto my land and spent the night in my fields, you must come along with me."

Giant Despair, therefore, took them to his castle and put them into a very dark, very dank, and very despicable dungeon. Here, then, the two pilgrims lay from Wednesday morning until Saturday night, without one bite of bread, or one drop of drink, or one flash of light, or anyone to ask how they were doing.

Now Giant Despair had a wife, and her name was Diffidence, the meaning of which is timidity or fear. After the giant had locked Christian and Hopeful in his dungeon, he told his wife what he had done and asked her what he should do with them in the future. When she found out who they were, she advised her husband to beat them without mercy in the morning.

And so he did, making a switch from the thorniest tree he could find. And the next morning he went down to the dungeon and, after verbally assaulting his two prisoners, he whipped them until they could hardly move. Then he left them for the day, leaving them to languish in their misery and pain.

That night he again asked his wife what to do. This time she suggested that he encourage the men to kill themselves. And so, the next morning, he went down to the dungeon and, seeing that they were still in pain from the day before, added insult to injury: "You men know you will never escape from this prison. So why don't you make things easy on yourselves and just end it all—I'll even supply you with the knife, the rope, or the poison. It's your choice."

The pilgrims, of course, pleaded for their release. This only made the giant more angry, and he refused to let them go. In the damp darkness the prospect of death suddenly didn't sound so bad.

And so, presently, Christian said to Hopeful, "Brother, what are we going to do? The life that we now live is miserable. For what it's worth, I don't know whether it is better to live like this or just give up and die. I think I would prefer death to life. The grave certainly seems better than this dungeon."

But Hopeful was quick to respond, "Indeed our present condition is terrible, and death would be far more welcome to me than to live here forever, but let us remember the promises of our Lord. For God, the One who made the world, may cause Giant Despair to die, or cause him to leave the door unlocked, such that we may escape. Whatever the case, my brother, let us be patient and endure for a while, for I am confident that the time will come for our release."

This counsel from Hopeful eased Christian's mind for the moment, and so they sat quietly in their sorrowful prison.

That evening, Giant Despair came to check on his prisoners, thinking they had probably already killed themselves. But, when he entered the dungeon, he found that they were still alive—although barely. In fact, having been starved for several days and severely beaten, they could hardly even breathe. Nonetheless, they were alive.

This, of course, enraged the giant who, before leaving with a huff, told them that because they had not taken his advice their treatment would grow even worse.

Night again came upon Doubting Castle, and as Giant Despair and Diffidence were talking she asked him about the prisoners, curious as to whether or not they had killed themselves yet.

"They are stubborn rogues," replied the giant. "They prefer to bear pain and hardship than to make an end of themselves."

"I know what you should do," his wife replied. "Tomorrow morning, take them into the castle yard and show them the bones and skulls of the last set of prisoners we caught. Tell them that, at the end of the week, you will tear them into pieces as you did with the previous group."

So that next morning, Giant Despair took Christian and Hopeful out of their dungeon and into the castle yard. As their eyes adjusted to the brightness, they saw several shallow graves.

"These are the remains of other pilgrims," the giant bellowed. "Like you, they also trespassed onto my property. And, when I thought the time was right, I tore them into pieces. And soon, I will do the same to you. Now get back in your dungeon!" And he threw them back into their underground prison. Horrified by their field trip, Christian and Hopeful lay there all day in lamentable silence.

Later that evening, the pilgrims in desperation began to pray— and they prayed for nearly the entire night. And, it was as they were praying that Christian, amazed at his forgetfulness, suddenly blurted out, "What a fool I am! Here I am lying in this stinking dungeon when I could be walking around freely! I have a key in my coat called Promise that will, I believe, open any lock in Doubting Castle."

"Wonderful," said Hopeful. "This is good news, Brother. Hurry and try it."

Then Christian pulled the key out of his coat and inserted it into the lock on the door. Immediately the lock gave way, and the door opened with ease. The pilgrims quickly fled from the dungeon and made their way to the door leading into the castle yard. Again the key opened the door. Then came the iron gate, and although the lock did not turn easily, it did turn.

So Christian and Hopeful thrust open the gate and hastily made their escape. And coming back to the King's highway, they erected a pillar in order to warn other pilgrims from falling prey to Giant Despair. Many, therefore, who came after Christian and Hopeful read the inscription and escaped danger.

And, as the two men continued on their journey, they sang:

When we left the King's highway all that we found,
Was treacherous, murderous, forbidden ground.

So may those who follow in our steps take care
Lest they also find themselves caught in Despair
But even if trapped in the darkest of jails
Cling to His Promise, whose word never fails.

SEEING LIFE THROUGH THE EYES OF FAITH

The imagery is clear enough. Because they were being tormented by doubt, despair, and fear, Christian and Hopeful found themselves almost ready to quit altogether. Yet, when they depended on God through prayer, they remembered God's promises—and their anguish was replaced with hope.

The same is true for us. Instead of giving in to doubt, we can stand on God's promises. Instead of succumbing to depression or worry, we can trust Him. Instead of being disheveled by what we see around us, we can be grounded in what we can't see—but what we know is true (Hebrews 11:1). It was the missionary Hudson Taylor who, in poverty, said, "We have twenty-five cents—and all the promises of God!"[4] May we also express that same level of hope-filled faith.

CHAPTER 26

THE LOVE HOPE PRODUCES

We always thank God, the Father of our Lord Jesus Christ, when we pray for you,
because we have heard of your faith in Christ Jesus and of the love you have for all the saints—
the faith and love that spring from the hope that is stored up for you in heaven
and that you have already heard about in the word of truth, the gospel.

COLOSSIANS 1:3–5

Our culture has a lot of ideas about what true love is. A quick survey reveals a plethora of possibilities: Love is never having to say you're sorry. Love is never having to say good-bye. Love is a battlefield. Love is having someone to share your life with. Love is in the air. Love is a feeling. Love is a game. Love is a drug. Love is pain. Love is the answer. Love is a rose. Love is grand. Love is in the stars. Love is forever. Love is all there is. And the list could go on and on.

The Bible, however, has a very different idea about what true love is (see 1 Corinthians 13:4–7). In Scripture, love is defined as selfless sacrifice, based more on volition than emotion. Of course, it also includes the emotional element; to say that the psalmist's love for God, for example, was void of emotion would be inaccurate (Psalm 42:1).

Nonetheless, in its most basic sense, biblical love is obedience to God (John 14:15) and service for others (Philippians 2:1–4). With this in mind, Jesus says that our highest priority should be to love God and then, secondly, to love others (Matthew 22:37–40).

The Christian virtues of hope and love are often paired in Scripture. In 1 Corinthians 13:7, we see that love "always hopes," and in Romans 12:12, sincere love is "joyful in hope." First Thessalonians 1:3 parallels the work of faith, the labor of love, and the endurance of hope as necessary counterparts. Paul even compares these virtues to pieces of armor, the breastplate being made up of faith and love, and the helmet consisting of hope (1 Thessalonians 5:8–9). And Colossians 1:5 simply states that love and faith "spring from the hope" that we have in Christ.

But how exactly does hope promote love in our lives? In what way do God's promises encourage us to obey Him and to serve others? The answer to these questions falls into two major categories—hope produces love for God and hope produces love for others.

1. Hope Produces Love for God. As we have already seen, the greatest commandment is that we would love God (see Deuteronomy 6:5). Jesus defines what that love looks like when He says, "If you love me, you will obey what I command" (John 14:15), and the apostle John writes, "This is love for God: to obey his commands. And his commands are not burdensome" (1 John 5:3). Simply stated, then, loving God—or obeying Him out of heartfelt gratitude and a genuine desire to glorify Him—is the most important thing we can do in this life. The Bible indicates that hope produces love for the Lord in several ways.

a. Hope motivates our love for the Lord as our Master and King. As our Master and King, Jesus has promised that He will return one day with His reward (2 Corinthians 5:10; Revelation 22:12). As a result, our goal is to win His approval (Galatians 1:10; 1 Peter 2:15) in order that we might be pleasing to Him. As His servants and His citizens, we hope greatly in the day that He comes back for us—a hope that heightens our love for Him because we can't wait for Him to arrive (2 Timothy 4:8).

As His citizens, we hope with great anticipation for the country we cannot yet see. Our hearts burst with nationalistic pride, not for the nations of this earth, but for the city of God. After all, this world is not our home (Hebrews 11:13; 1 Peter 1:1, 2:11). We are simply passing through—traveling to the home we love even though we've not yet been there (Philippians 3:20; Ephesians 2:19). Our fondness is not for the things of this earth because our hearts are set on the place prepared for us by Christ. And it truly is the love we have for our King that ignites within us the desperate longing for His kingdom.

Our affection, then, is not defined by the short-lived glitter of this planet. It is determined by the eternal glories of God Himself, for we are those who "seek first his kingdom" (Matthew 6:33). He alone is the essence of all we love and the epitome of all we desire. He is what makes heaven so glorious—He is the heartbeat of our hope (see 1 Peter 1:8). And we are strengthened by His promise that we will one day be with Him in the glorious splendor of His palace. Although we are presently aliens and strangers, we are not without a home; the King whom we love has promised us a place in His house (John 14:2).

b. Hope motivates our love for the Lord as our Shepherd and Father. Beyond servants and citizens, Scripture also describes believers as both sheep and children. The Shepherd whom we follow is "the good shepherd" (John 10:11). And the Father who adopted us is a loving Father. So, when we hope in God's goodness and guidance, we see His faithfulness. The result, in us, is greater trust. And since love is built on trust, it too is heightened by hope.

Psalm 23 is probably the most well-known account of God's love for us as our Shepherd. Because He is our Shepherd, we can trust in His provision (v. 1), His leading (vv. 2–3), His safekeeping (v. 4), and

His blessing (vv. 5–6). His promise, of course, is that He will take care of us. When we hope in that promise and follow Him, we demonstrate that we love Him.

And, as our perfect Father, God adopts us into His family and promises us an inheritance with Christ. While our love is not based on the hope of that inheritance, it is nonetheless deepened by the generosity of our Father. It is no understatement when John exclaims, "How great is the love the Father has lavished on us, that we should be called children of God!" (1 John 3:1). Our love for Him, then, should be like the love of a child as we recognize our total dependence on Him. He has promised to take care of us in both this life and the next. How can we not respond with gratitude and devotion?

Our familial relationship is not just provisional, but also personal. Romans 8:15 says that, based on our adoption, we can call God "Abba," a term of intimate affection between a child and a father. The hope of eternity, then, is not a stark existence in the holy halls of heaven. Our hope is in an everlasting love that we will share with our Father—a love that starts in this life and grows into the next.

c. We love the Lord as the Bridegroom of the church. As the church's bridegroom, Jesus promises to one day bring all believers to Himself, in perfect fellowship, for all eternity. In light of this, when we hope in one day being with our Savior, we are moved with love for Him. Such a longing is not wishful thinking. It is not a fantastic fairy tale. It is an affection built on hope—a love based firmly on the promises of God. We have yet to even see our Savior, yet He is already our best friend, the culmination of everything we hold dear.

The saying "Absence makes the heart grow fonder" should definitely be true of us. Unfortunately, for many Christians, it is just the opposite. Christ's absence has allowed our hearts to grow cold and to look for satisfaction in the things of this earth. Yet, the promise of His return, the promise of being with Him forever, the promise of eternally finding our satisfaction in Him—these are promises that rekindle our love and our passion for the Savior. As His followers, we should set our hearts steadfastly on Him, firmly grounding our love in our hope.

As our Master, King, Shepherd, Father, and Bridegroom—in each of these ways, hope motivates our love for the Lord. His promises remind us to look to Him with eager affection and to obey Him from a sincere heart.

2. Hope Produces Love for Others. Biblical love also looks for ways to sacrificially serve others. In fact, 1 John 4:7–8 says that if we truly love God we will love other people too. Jesus put it this way, "By this all men will know that you are my disciples, if you love one another" (John 13:35). And, although love can be faked, Romans 12:9 commands Christians to love sincerely, without hypocrisy. Here are three ways in which hope produces genuine love for other people.

a. Hope motivates Christians to serve one another. Hope produces sacrificial service for others because it longs for God's reward. In Philippians 2:1–4, Paul commands his readers to put the interests of others above their own. But some may wonder: "What about what I deserve? What about my recognition?" Hope responds to such questions by reminding us that God is always watching, and He will reward us for our faithfulness.

Once we realize that our goal is not to please ourselves, but to please God, service becomes a lot easier. You can set up chairs for Sunday school, even if no one notices, because your reward is in heaven. You can loan money to a friend and never be repaid, because your riches are not of this earth. You can exhaust yourself in ministry and not complain, because you know eternal rest is coming. In other words, loving His people is not about being loved in return. Instead, it's about pleasing Him (see 1 Peter 1:21–22; 3:8–9).

b. Hope motivates Christians to encourage one another. A second major component of true love is encouragement—building up other people with the truth and strengthening their hearts. When others around us begin to feel discouraged or downcast, biblical love cheers their countenance by reminding them of God's goodness and care (1 Thessalonians 5:14).

There is no better way to encourage the fainthearted than to graciously remind them of God's promises—our hope. In 1 Thessalonians 5:8, 11, Paul commands his readers to put on "the hope of salvation as a helmet" and then to "encourage one another and build each other up." And the author of Hebrews tells believers to "hold unswervingly to the hope we profess" and to use that hope to "encourage one another—and all the more as you see the Day approaching" (Hebrews 10:23, 25). With this in mind, Christians should urge others to keep their focus on God's perfect promises, finding their comfort in Him rather than anywhere else.

c. Hope motivates Christians to reach out to the lost. While we are to serve and encourage other believers, our love must not stay trapped inside the walls of our home or our church. We are to love unbelievers, too—primarily by sharing the truth of God's Word with them through both our words and our lives. Even when they respond with hatred and persecution, our love for them should be undaunted.

Hope plays a major part in our love for unbelievers. After all, the message of the gospel is the message of hope. The offer of salvation is based on God's promise. As 1 Peter 3:15 says, we should always be ready to tell others about the hope that we have. And sincere love not only witnesses verbally, but also through kind acts and sacrificial deeds.

When the response is less than friendly, Scripture says we should rejoice, because our reward in heaven will be great (Luke 6:35–36; Acts 5:41; 1 Peter 3:14). In light of this, the hope of our glorious future not only motivates us to tell others about it but also enables us to respond with patience and graciousness when unbelievers do not want to hear.

HOW'S YOUR LOVE LIFE?

For the Christian, then, love for God and love for others is the summation of our duty (Matthew 22:36–40). When we fail to love, we are failing in every area of our Christian lives. Yet, the promises of God can help stimulate our love: by reminding us of what is truly important, by taking our eyes off of ourselves, by focusing our attention on God and His reward, and by assuring us that we can empty ourselves in this life because we will have perfect rest in the next.

While most people in the world are confused about what love is, Christians should be known as those who exhibit true love. Jesus Himself said that this is how the world would know us. But the selfish pursuits of today can only be sacrificed for the good of others when we realize that, in the long run, the things of this earth are not what matter. Only God, His Word, and people are eternal. Our goal should be to love the things that will last and put our energies there, rather than wasting our time on what is passing away.

CHAPTER 27

THE WORLD'S FIRST SAILOR:
The Results of Hope in the Life of Noah

By faith Noah, when warned about things not yet seen,
in holy fear built an ark to save his family.
By his faith he condemned the world and became heir of
the righteousness that comes by faith.

HEBREWS 11:7

My earliest memories include the stories of great biblical heroes, usually presented as flannel-graph characters or picture-Bible portraits. There were Adam and Eve, Cain and Abel, Jacob and Esau, Joseph and his brothers, and a myriad of others. I loved listening to how Samson defeated a lion with his bare hands, how Jonathan protected his best friend David, and how Esther convinced her husband to spare the Jews. In every story, the point was always the same—God is faithful to those who hope in Him.

In the next three chapters, we will look at the lives of three men who put their hope in God. Certainly, these men were not perfect; they were sinners just like everybody else. Yet, the general pattern of each of their lives was righteousness and confident trust. Despite seemingly impossible odds, they looked to God for help and deliverance—and He never failed them. So, although they accomplished some amazing feats, all of the glory goes to the One in whom they found their strength—namely, God alone.

A MAN NAMED NOAH

The first individual we will consider is Noah—the man famous for building the ark. Almost everyone, even outside of the church, knows about Noah. His animal-filled boat has found its way into greeting cards, baby decorations, comic strips, and even movie theaters. Of course, most people would categorize Noah as more of a mythic legend than a factual figure, yet the tales of his enormous boat and a catastrophic flood have captured the imaginations of many.

The Bible, on the other hand, presents Noah as a literal, historical character, explaining the events of his life as actual occurrences. Even Jesus speaks of Noah in a factual sense (Matthew 24:37–38), never once suggesting that the Genesis stories were fabricated or make-believe. What, then, can we learn from this man of God who lived thousands of years ago? While certainly not an exhaustive list, here are four lessons that we can take from Noah's hope-filled life.

1. You Can Hope in God Even When His Promise Seems Unpleasant. When Noah was born, the earth was actually quite different than it is now. Instead of seven continents and a myriad of islands, the land was concentrated in one large mass (see 1 Chronicles 1:19). Instead of steep mountains and deep canyons, the landscape was more gentle and rolling. Instead of harmful ultraviolet rays and global warming, the earth's atmosphere was protected by a dense firmament—possibly of ice or thick clouds (Genesis 1:7, 7:11–12). And, instead of rain, the lush vegetation was supported by streams, or mists, that came up from the ground (Genesis 2:6).

The flood, of course, dramatically changed all of this. But Noah was born before the flood, meaning that the world he knew for most of his life was the closest this planet has ever come to utopia, outside of the Garden of Eden.

Not everything was perfect, however. Although the earth was teeming with life, men and women had utterly rebelled against God. In fact, the situation was so bad that God looked down from heaven and said, "I will wipe mankind, whom I have created, from the face of the earth—men and animals, and creatures that move along the ground, and birds of the air—for I am grieved that I have made them" (Genesis 6:7). Only Noah found favor in God's sight.

So God came to Noah and told him the news, saying, "I am going to bring floodwaters on the earth to destroy all life under the heavens, every creature that has the breath of life in it. Everything on earth will perish. But I will establish my covenant with you, and you will enter the ark—you and your sons and your wife and your sons' wives with you" (Genesis 6:17–18).

Certainly, Noah was happy to be spared from coming judgment. And, as a righteous man (Genesis 6:9), he was surely offended by the idolatrous and immoral lives of the other people he knew. Yet, the news probably evoked a mixed emotion—the beautiful world that Noah had known was going to be destroyed; only his family and a representative pair of every kind of animal would survive. Learning about the flood, for Noah, would be like our learning that a nuclear war was soon to break out.

Nonetheless, Noah did not respond with doubt or complaint. The text simply says, "Noah did everything just as God commanded him" (Genesis 6:22). Even though God's promised judgment sounded extreme, Noah trusted that God knew what He was doing. Instead of arguing or becoming depressed, Noah chose to believe and to obey. Noah knew that the God he served was infinitely wise and perfectly just. So, he hoped in the Lord even though God's promise was unpleasant.

2. You Can Hope in God Even When His Promise Is Unpopular. As might be expected, when Noah told others about God's unpleasant promise it wasn't well received by the society of his day. Yet, Noah continued to hope in God even though it meant that he was unpopular. Even while everyone around him was ignoring him and going about their daily routines as if nothing was wrong (Matthew 24:38), Noah continued to faithfully warn them as a "preacher of righteousness" (2 Peter 2:5).

It's not hard to imagine why his message would be so poorly received. Here is a man building a gigantic boat, warning of a worldwide flood, and it's never even rained before. His friends and neighbors must have thought he was crazy. And as his project grew closer and closer to completion, it presumably attracted a larger and larger crowd, as people from all around came to see the "lunatic" and his massive ship.

Presumably, Noah was mocked, ridiculed, and despised. At the very least, his message was rejected by all who heard it. After all, only he and his family were saved. Nevertheless, Noah remained faithful. He chose to obey God and to proclaim the Lord's message, not because it was popular, but because it was true. Clearly, Noah preferred to hope in God's promises than to be silenced by the desire for public acceptance.

3. You Can Hope in God Even When His Promise Is Unhurried. Not only did Noah hope in God when His promise was unpleasant and unpopular, but also when the fulfillment of that promise was slow in coming. In fact, it was 120 years from the time God decided that He would destroy the earth until the time He actually sent the flood (Genesis 6:3). No wonder the people of Noah's day thought he was crazy; the destruction he kept talking about seemed like it was never coming.

Interestingly, skeptics today respond the same way to the hope we have of Christ's return. "He's never coming back," they taunt. "It's already been two thousand years. If He were going to come, He'd have been here by now." The apostle Peter responds to this very issue in 2 Peter 3:3–10, reminding modern skeptics not to make the same mistake as the skeptics of Noah's day. Just because God is patient doesn't mean His promises will never be fulfilled. Rather than living in expectation, the victims of the flood were taken by surprise—simply ignoring Noah's warning until God's judgment caught up with them (Matthew 24:38; Luke 17:26–27).

For us, as Christians, the certainty of future fulfillment—even if it is still a long way off—should be immensely encouraging. No matter how long we have to wait, we can be confident that Jesus will return and that we will receive everything we have been promised. In the meantime, realizing that Christ may return at any moment, we should be faithful to obey as we trust His timing (see 2 Peter 3:11–13).

4. You Can Hope in God Even When Your Future Is Unknown. A fourth lesson that Noah's life teaches us about hope is that we can trust God's promises even when our future is unknown and seemingly uncertain. At least five times in Noah's life, he was forced to trust God because he had no idea what the future held. The first time came when God told him the flood was coming. Imagine what Noah must have thought. It had never rained before—so Noah must have wondered what the coming rains of judgment would be like.

Second, he was commanded to build a massive boat. What would his friends and neighbors think? What kind of reputation would he be making for himself? Questions like these would have naturally come to his mind. Yet, despite the fact that he did not know what would happen, Noah simply trusted God and obeyed His commands.

Third, once the rain began to fall and the floodwaters began to rise, Noah had to continue to trust God for his safety and survival. Noah had no idea what the flood itself would be like—except to know that it would be catastrophic. He could not even begin to imagine the torrential downpour, the enormous waves, the incredible winds. Yet, because he believed God's promise, he boarded the ark with his family, confident that God had everything under control.

Then, fourth, after the waters began to recede, Noah had no way of knowing what the postflood world would be like. Certainly, it would be different. At the very least, he knew that all of the wicked people who had been alive would be gone. But how would he and his family survive? All of the earth's crops had been destroyed, and the only animals alive were with him in the ark. Much of the world was still covered in water. For most of us, the worry and anxiety would have been overwhelming. Yet, for Noah, he trusted God (see Genesis 8:15–20).

Finally, even after he and his family had disembarked and were safely on dry ground, Noah continued to trust the Lord. After having witnessed and lived through the judgment of God, Noah might have been worried that a similar catastrophe could strike again. God, however, promised to never flood the entire earth again (Genesis 9:12–17). Instead of living in anxiety and fear, Noah accepted God's promise in faith. God's covenant, in the form of a rainbow, was more than enough to put Noah's mind at ease.

You Can Have Hope like Noah

All of us have experienced times when the storms of life seem to cloud out any light and drown any joy. For Noah, his storm was literal. Yet, instead of putting his eyes on the beautiful world around him or on his own reputation and safety, he chose to look to God's promise.

Though the promised judgment of God was unpleasant, unpopular, and unhurried, Noah knew it was coming because God said it was coming. And while his future was unknown, at least to him, Noah continued to trust God—from the time the first nail was pounded into the ark to the time he walked out onto a completely changed landscape.

As we look at Noah's life, we can be encouraged to know that the God who kept His promises to Noah is the same God who keeps His word today. When hardship and difficulty come into our lives, we can trust in His wisdom and love. When we receive persecution and ridicule for proclaiming His message, we can rejoice in looking forward to His reward. And when we are confused about what the future holds, we can hope in the fact that God is in control.

So the next time you see a card with a cartoon Noah on the front or enter a kid's room with the ark stenciled on the wall, remember the lessons of Noah's life. Instead of hoping in the pleasures of his society, he chose to live righteously. Instead of ignoring God's warning, he chose to build the ark. Instead of wondering what was taking so long, he chose to rely on God's timing. Instead of fretting about surviving the flood, he chose to trust God for his safety. And instead of fearing that the flood might recur, he decided to rest in the promise of God. For Noah, the sign of God's promise was the rainbow. For us, when we see that sign, we can remind ourselves, "The God of hope put that rainbow there. He kept His promise to Noah. He'll keep His promises to me."

CHAPTER 28

THE FATHER OF A NATION:

The Results of Hope in the Life of Abraham

Against all [human] hope, Abraham in hope believed and so became the father of many nations,
. . .being fully persuaded that God had power to do what he had promised.

ROMANS 4:18, 21

Abraham is one of the most famous and beloved Bible characters of all time. His story, which is told in Genesis 11–25, has been retold countless times—from the rabbis of Old Testament Israel to the Sunday school teachers of today. He has been the subject of songs, sermons, books, and theological discussions. In fact, both the Jews and the Arabs look to him as their physical ancestor. Indeed, God kept His promise to Abraham when He told him, "I will make your name great" (Genesis 12:2).

It's easy for us, four thousand years later, to take Abraham's life for granted. We've heard the stories so many times, and we know how everything is going to turn out. Yet, in contrast to us, Abraham did not have the luxury of knowing how the story was going to end. Instead, he simply had to trust God for what the future would hold. As each situation arose, he was forced to make a decision: Will I hope in God and trust Him, or will I do things my own way?

As with all of us, there were times when Abraham did not hope in God as he should have (see Genesis 20). Nevertheless, on the whole, Abraham's life was characterized by a steadfast faith in God's promises. Even when the fulfillment of those promises went far beyond his own lifetime, Abraham's settled confidence motivated him to simply trust and obey. Here are four lessons that Abraham's life teaches us about hope.

1. You Can Hope in God's Perfect Plan. The year was approximately 2091 B.C. Abraham (who was then called "Abram") was seventy-five years old. He was living in the town of Haran, where he had moved, along with his father, from his birthplace, Ur. Geographically speaking, Haran was located in northeastern Mesopotamia (modern-day Iraq), just east of the Euphrates River.

Abraham had grown up in a pagan family, as Joshua 24:2 records. Being from Ur, he had probably been raised as a worshiper of the Sumerian moon god Nannar, also called Sin. Abraham's own father, Terah, was probably named after this deity—his name being derived from the Hebrew word for moon.[1]

Josephus tells us that Abraham was, in fact, a great astronomer.[2] When God saved him, he realized that stars and the planets were not gods in and of themselves, but simply created bodies, operating according to the design of the Creator. After his conversion, Abraham quickly began to denounce the astrology of his neighbors by telling them about the true God. Naturally, his neighbors weren't too happy that Abraham was condemning their pagan worship. His faithful proclamations were met with what Josephus calls a "tumult" of opposition.

It is in this context then that God told Abraham to move his family to Canaan, promising to make his descendants into a great nation (Genesis 12:1–3). What a promise! Yet, for Abraham, it meant leaving behind everything he had known for his whole life.

The place where he was comfortable, the place where his father had died, the place where he had settled. Moreover, it tested whether he truly believed in the God about whom he had been telling others. Surely, it would have been easier to just stay in Haran, keep his mouth shut about religion, and mind his own business. Most likely, he had never been to Canaan, the land which the Lord promised him—and now God wanted him to just get up and move?

But Abraham didn't ask questions or make excuses. He didn't drag his feet or complain (see Genesis 12:4–5). Instead, he chose to trust the God he knew was faithful, focusing on God's promise rather than his own comfort or agenda. He placed his confidence in God's plan, knowing that the Lord would send him exactly where he needed to be. While his own preference may have been to stay in Haran, Abraham obeyed God's command—knowing that the Lord's will was best even if it meant a total life change.

2. You Can Hope in God's Perfect Justice. Upon settling in the land of Canaan, Abraham and his nephew Lot decided to part ways because their herds of livestock were getting too large to keep together. In his graciousness, Abraham gave his nephew first choice as to where he would raise his flocks. So Lot selected the most fertile land for himself, the land surrounding Sodom and Gomorrah.

Yet, greener grass was not the better choice because Sodom, Lot's main residence (Genesis 13:12–13), proved to be an incredibly perverse city. In fact, it was so wicked that God decided to destroy it and the surrounding towns on account of its rampant immorality.

When Abraham learned of the Lord's intention, he interceded for the city—asking that God might spare Sodom on account of any righteous people living there (Genesis 18:20–33). After all, it was home for his nephew Lot. Presumably, he knew others in the city too—because in Genesis 14:1–16, Abraham had rescued Sodom's inhabitants when it had been invaded. And so, Abraham pleaded on the city's behalf, and God assured him that even if there were only ten righteous people in the city, He would not destroy it (Genesis 18:32).

Having received God's assurance, Abraham was content to trust the perfect justice of the Lord. While he could not be sure what would happen to Sodom, as to whether it would be spared, Abraham knew that he could rest in God's righteous judgment. The Lord Himself had promised that He would not destroy Sodom unnecessarily. He would not be haphazard in dispensing His wrath.

In Genesis 19 we learn that there was only one righteous person in Sodom, namely, Lot (2 Peter 2:7). So, although Lot was rescued, Sodom was destroyed. Yet, Abraham's intercession proved that He knew God to be a patient executioner; One who wielded His anger carefully and not without just cause.

Abraham's hope in God's perfect judgment is evident, in Genesis 18:25, when he says to the Lord, "Far be it from you to do such a thing—to kill the righteous with the wicked, treating the righteous and the wicked alike. Far be it from you! Will not the Judge of all the earth do right?" Abraham's confidence in God's justice allowed him to trust that, even in punishment, the right thing would be done.

As Christians, it is sometimes hard for us to understand how a loving God can punish sinners—both in this life and the next. Like Abraham, however, we can trust that the Judge of all the earth will do what is right. His wisdom is faultless and His judgments are pure. So, while we plead for those around us, in the end, we can rest in God's perfect justice.

3. You Can Hope in God's Perfect Timing. In Genesis 17, God promised Abraham that he would have a son, through his wife, Sarah. At the time, however, both Abraham and Sarah were very old, and Sarah had been barren her whole life. Nevertheless, God's promise was clear: "I will bless her [Sarah] and will surely give you a son by her. I will bless her so that she will be the mother of nations;

kings of peoples will come from her" (Genesis 17:16). In fact, when the Lord visited Abraham in chapter 18, He reiterated this guarantee: "I will surely return to you about this time next year, and Sarah your wife will have a son" (v. 10).

Sarah's response, when she heard what God said, was probably the same response that many of us would have had. She laughed in disbelief, thinking she was far too old (Genesis 17:11–12). Abraham, too, had initially responded with doubt-filled laughter (see Genesis 17:17–18). Yet, Hebrews 11:11 indicates that his disposition soon changed to one of confident hope: "By faith Abraham, even though he was past age—and Sarah herself was barren—was enabled to become a father because he considered him faithful who had made the promise." Paul echoes this description in Romans 4:18–21. Even when childbearing seemed physically impossible, Abraham chose to believe God's promises rather than to focus on the scientific impossibilities of his situation. And God was faithful (see Genesis 21:1–2).

In fact, God always keeps His word—a lesson that Abraham and Sarah obviously learned. Even their son's name, Isaac (meaning "laughter"), pointed both to their initial disbelief in God's promise and the subsequent joy they found in His faithfulness. They thought they were too old to have children, but God wanted them to trust His perfect timing. And, in learning to hope in God regarding Isaac's birth, Abraham was later able to trust Him when Isaac was nearly killed.

4. You Can Hope in God's Perfect Wisdom. In Genesis 22, God decided to test Abraham's loyalty, to see exactly where his hope had truly been placed. So, in verse 2, God said to Abraham, "Take your son, your only son, Isaac, whom you love, and go to the region of Moriah. Sacrifice him there as a burnt offering on one of the mountains I will tell you about."

I can only imagine what Abraham must have thought when he heard those words—maybe something like: *What is going on? This is the son that You gave us, Lord, in our old age. When we thought there was no hope of having children, You gave us this boy. Your promise to me, about being the father of a great nation, is based on this child. He is the descendant that makes it all possible. And now You want me to kill him? This can't be right. There must be some mistake.*

Yet, God had already proven His faithfulness to Abraham in the birth of their son. So, when asked to do the seemingly unthinkable, Abraham responded with confident trust and without complaint.

As he and Isaac approached the place for the sacrifice, Isaac noticed that something was wrong. So he asked his father, "The fire and wood are here, but where is the lamb for the burnt offering?" Abraham's hope-filled reply was simply, "God himself will provide" (Genesis 22:7–8). Just minutes later, when they reached the designated spot, Abraham tied up his son and prepared the sacrifice. What could he have been thinking at this moment? Hebrews 11:17–19 tells us:

> *By faith Abraham, when God tested him, offered Isaac as a sacrifice. He who had received the promises was about to sacrifice his one and only son, even though God had said to him, "It is through Isaac that your offspring will be reckoned." Abraham reasoned that God could raise the dead, and figuratively speaking, he did receive Isaac back from death.*

Abraham was so confident in God's promises that he figured, even if he killed his son, God would raise him back up from the dead. Talk about faith! Since God had promised to raise up a great nation through Isaac (Genesis 15:5–21), Abraham knew He would keep His word.

In Genesis 22:12–14, God stops Abraham from killing his son, instead providing a ram, caught in a nearby thicket, for the sacrifice. Isaac's life was spared. Yet, Abraham had demonstrated that he was willing to give up everything for God, including his own child. Through his actions, he had shown that God's promises were what dictated his behavior. His priorities and perspective were right because they focused on God rather than anything else.

YOU CAN HAVE A HOPE LIKE ABRAHAM'S

At every major point of Abraham's life, he chose to trust God even when the future was uncertain. When he could have stayed in Haran, he chose instead to hope in God's plan and direction. When he feared for the safety of the righteous in Sodom, he chose to hope in God's perfect justice. When he thought it impossible to have a child through his wife, Sarah, he chose to believe God's promise. And when he was asked to slay his son Isaac, he trusted God's wisdom, demonstrating that he was willing to obey any command God gave.

In each of these decisions, Abraham put his hope in God even though he did not know what the outcome would be. Hebrews 6:13–15 says this:

> *When God made his promise to Abraham, since there was no one greater for him to swear by, he swore by himself, saying, "I will surely bless you and give you many descendants." And so after waiting patiently, Abraham received what was promised.*

Simply put, Abraham hoped in God's promises simply because God gave them, and there is no one more trustworthy than God. As spiritual descendants of Abraham (Romans 4:16), we should share a similar confidence in our great Savior! He has given us His promises. All we have to do is trust and obey.

CHAPTER 29

THE MAN AFTER
GOD'S OWN HEART:
The Results of Hope in the Life of David

Find rest, O my soul, in God alone;
my hope comes from him.
He alone is my rock and my salvation;
he is my fortress, I will not be shaken.

PSALM 62:5–6

Born the youngest son of a commoner, David's rise to power is truly a testimony of God's grace. A shepherd boy with seven older brothers, David could have never dreamed of one day being king of Israel. But that is exactly what God had in store for him. And so, while David was still a boy, the prophet Samuel came and anointed him as the future king (1 Samuel 16:13).

At the time, of course, King Saul was still in power. Yet, because of Saul's continual disobedience, God decided to take the throne away from him (1 Samuel 15:28) and give it, instead, to a man whose mind was devoted to the things of the Lord. David was that man. As God told Samuel in 1 Samuel 16:7, "The LORD does not look at the things man looks at. Man looks at the outward appearance, but the

LORD looks at the heart." Simply put, God was looking for a man after His own heart (1 Samuel 13:14; Acts 13:22).

While David's heart was certainly in the right place, his life was not always free of trouble. In fact, he faced numerous trials and difficulties—times in which his life was in danger or his feelings deeply hurt. Nevertheless, through it all, he kept his focus on the promises of God, relying on the strength of his sovereign Lord. As a man known for his intimate relationship with God, he leaves a profound legacy for us to follow after. Here are four lessons you can learn from the life of David.

1. You Can Hope in God When the Odds Seem Impossible. Shortly after Samuel's visit to David's family, the army of the nearby Philistines came to wage war with Israel. The fact that the Philistines were attacking was not unusual, for Israel had long been enemies with their western neighbors. But this time there was something different—the Philistine army had a secret weapon.

Standing over nine feet tall, Goliath of Gath was certainly a notable warrior. His polished shield, sparkling helmet, and sharpened sword made him look even more impressive. Towering over everyone he met, even our tallest basketball players would have only come to his shoulder. Needless to say, this giant was the pride of Philistia—a true champion of massive proportions.

No wonder the army of Israel was intimidated when they faced the Philistines some twenty miles southwest of Jerusalem. No wonder they cowered in fear when Goliath shouted his challenge across the valley floor: "Give me a man and let us fight each other" (1 Samuel 17:10). Obviously, no one in Saul's army wanted to take up the challenge.

It was this scene that the young David encountered when he came to the front lines with provisions for his older brothers. What he found alarmed him with disappointment—the soldiers of Israel were paralyzed with terror.

Deciding something must be done, David went to King Saul and announced that he would fight Goliath. Saul probably laughed to himself when he heard it. His reply was simple, "You are not able to go out against this Philistine and fight him; you are only a boy, and he has been a fighting man from his youth" (1 Samuel 17:33). But Saul had no one else willing to go. And David's courage remained undeterred. "The LORD," said David with confidence, "will deliver me from the hand of this Philistine" (1 Samuel 17:37). Saul reluctantly agreed.

When David finally went out to meet his giant opponent, having declined the armor Saul offered, all Goliath could do was mock. Were the Israelites really sending a shepherd boy to fight on their behalf? In disbelief, Goliath taunted, "Am I a dog, that you come at me with sticks?" (1 Samuel 17:43).

David's reply (1 Samuel 17:45, 47) was classic:

> *"You come against me with sword and spear and javelin, but I come against you in the name of the LORD Almighty. . .for the battle is the LORD'S, and he will give all of you into our hands."*

What confidence this mere teenager expressed in the face of seemingly unbeatable odds. What a contrast he was to the army of his countrymen. What courage he had, not in his own ability, but rather in the power of his God.

We all know the story. David used his slingshot to kill his foe with a well-placed stone to Goliath's forehead. We've all heard the Sunday school lessons and watched the cartoon depictions. But don't let familiarity with the story breed indifference to the overwhelming hope of the young David. Because his focus was on God and God's glory, his foe seemed insignificant. Who is Goliath, he must have wondered, if the Lord is on my side? A mere man, no matter how tall or intimidating, is nothing compared to the God of the universe (see Romans 8:31).

Often we, like Israel's army, choose to fear men and circumstances more than we fear God. But it is only when we change our focus, looking at the greatness of the King we serve, that we can have the right perspective. After all, even our biggest problems are small in comparison to His power. Our God is great and we can hope in Him.

2. You Can Hope in God When the Wait Seems Unbearable. After David defeated Goliath, his fame in Israel instantly spread. As a result, King Saul began to grow jealous (1 Samuel 18:8–9), worried that David would be the one to take his throne away from him. Even after David married his daughter, Saul was still on edge (1 Samuel 18:28–29), because David's military success and public popularity continued to increase. So King Saul decided that David must be killed—meaning that from 1 Samuel 19 until Saul's death in 1 Samuel 31:6, David was forced to live as a fugitive, constantly running for his life.

Two occasions are especially significant during this time in David's life, both of them involving his near-capture by Saul. The first is recorded in 1 Samuel 24:1–22. Saul's army had been pursuing David when they came to a place where the hillsides were dotted with caves. Little did Saul know that David and his men were actually hiding in one of the caverns. And so, needing a place to rest, the king ventured into the very cave where David and his men were hiding.

David's followers encouraged him to kill King Saul while he had the chance. But, David would do no such thing. He simply replied, "The LORD forbid that I should do such a thing to my master, the LORD's anointed, or lift my hand against him; for he is the anointed of the LORD" (1 Samuel 24:6). In other words, David trusted God's timing rather than his own. He knew that God would end Saul's life when God was ready to do so. In the meantime, David was not going to rush things on account of his own selfish desires.

First Samuel 26:1–25 gives a similar account. Saul again is chasing

David and David again has an opportunity to take the king's life. Once more, David chooses to trust God's timing rather than his own. In verse 10, David says, "As surely as the LORD lives. . .the LORD himself will strike him; either his time will come and he will die, or he will go into battle and perish." David knew that God was in control and that God would remove Saul when the time was right. Instead of manipulating his way to the throne, David rested in God's plan.

What would you have done in David's situation? Would you have been able to trust God's timing—even if it meant postponing your kingship and letting the man who was trying to kill you go free? David did, because he knew his God was faithful, and he was confident that he could put his hope in Him.

3. You Can Hope in God Even After You've Sinned. Many years later, long after Saul was dead and David had been crowned king, David made a tragic wrong choice—one that was not typical of this godly man.

It was springtime and, instead of going out to war with his army as was customary, David for some reason decided to stay home (2 Samuel 11:1). One evening, while he was walking around on the roof of his palace, David looked down at a nearby house and saw a woman bathing outside. Instead of turning away, like he should have, David chose to yield to his lust. Instead of running from the situation, David invited the woman to come to the palace. And instead of sending her back home when he learned she was married, David committed adultery with her.

Some days later, the woman—whose name was Bathsheba—realized that she was pregnant. Since her husband, Uriah, was away in David's army, it was clear that David was the father. Hoping to cover things up, David quickly brought Uriah home from the battle so that it would seem like the baby was his. But Uriah refused to even sleep in his own house, arguing that he could not enjoy the comforts of home while his friends were still on the front line (2 Samuel 11:11).

So, David sent him back to the army and arranged to have him killed (2 Samuel 11:15–17).

Lust, adultery, falsehood, and murder—it's hard to believe that King David was even capable of such atrocities. And then, instead of repenting right away, he tried to hide it, marrying Bathsheba shortly after Uriah's death (2 Samuel 11:27). But God knew what had happened. And so He sent Nathan, His prophet, to rebuke King David for his sin (see 2 Samuel 12:1–12).

According to Jewish tradition, David penned Psalm 51 shortly after repenting of his sin with Bathsheba. Accepting full responsibility for his actions and expressing his willingness to pay the full penalty, David leaned on God's goodness for mercy. He says this in verse 1: "Have mercy on me, O God, according to your unfailing love; according to your great compassion blot out my transgressions." Realizing that his sin was first and foremost against God (v. 4), David found consolation in God's infinite grace and perfect justice.

David could have tried to deny his sin, but he knew that no one can hide anything from God. So instead, he chose to hope in God's unfailing love. And while he understood that there were still consequences to pay, he was confident that his sin had been forgiven.

As Christians, we can also hope in God's forgiveness. Because of Jesus' sacrifice, believers can be certain that their sins have been covered by His blood. No sin is so great that God's grace is not greater still. As it did with David, sin often comes with consequences. Yet, we can rest assured that, through Christ, our sins have been pardoned.

4. You Can Hope in God Even When Life Hurts. The remainder of David's life was full of hardship and trouble. It began with the death of Bathsheba's baby boy in 2 Samuel 12:15–23. Then, in 2 Samuel 13:1–22, David's son Amnon raped David's daughter Tamar—Tamar was Amnon's half sister. When David refused to avenge Tamar's humiliation, his son Absalom, Tamar's full brother, murdered Amnon (2 Samuel 13:23–29). Even after David pardoned

Absalom for his actions (2 Samuel 14:25–33), Absalom turned on his father and led a rebellion against him (2 Samuel 15:1–18:18). Although the mutiny failed, and David's kingship survived, he was greatly grieved when Absalom was killed (2 Samuel 18:33). To add to his troubles, a second rebellion, although short-lived, broke out soon thereafter under a man named Sheba (2 Samuel 20:1–22). Needless to say, David had his share of difficulties.

As expected, the pain of all these events was very real—causing David deep times of personal grief and almost uncontrollable weeping. His fractured family and treason-prone kingdom caused him incredible heartache. Yet, at the end of it all, in 2 Samuel 22, David demonstrates that his hope was still in the Lord. In verses 47, 50–51, he writes:

> *"The LORD lives! Praise be to my Rock! Exalted be God, the Rock, my Savior! . . . Therefore I will praise you, O LORD, among the nations; I will sing praises to your name. He gives his king great victories; he shows unfailing kindness to his anointed, to David and his descendants forever."*

At the end of all the pain he had endured, David still found his strength in the Lord. Although, on occasion, he had failed God, God had never failed Him. He could have looked back on his failures and his sorrow and been discouraged. Instead, he put his hope in the King of heaven, thanking Him for His kindness and mercy.

Like David, our lives are often full of disappointment, sadness, grief, and pain. Sometimes it is the result of our own failure. Sometimes it is caused by outside sources. Whatever the case, we must remember to find our strength in God. If we look anywhere else, we are sure to be overwhelmed. Even when life hurts, our only hope is the Lord.

You Can Have a Hope like David

In Psalm 145:13, David exclaims, "The LORD is faithful to all his promises and loving toward all he has made." Hope in God's promises—that certainly was the heart cry of the man after God's own heart. He trusted God's power, even when Goliath stood in his way. He trusted God's timing, even when Saul was trying to take his life. He trusted God's mercy, even after he had committed grievous sin. And he trusted God's sovereign grace, even when everything around him seemed to be crumbling. The promises of God were precious to David. He hoped in them even when his circumstances seemed impossible. When we build our lives on God's promises, we too can echo David's words, "Find rest, O my soul, in God alone; my hope comes from him" (Psalm 62:5).

CHAPTER 30

THE PLACE TO LOOK:

Where to Go When Searching for Hope

"Man is a mere phantom as he goes to and fro: He bustles about, but only in vain;
he heaps up wealth, not knowing who will get it.
But now, Lord, what do I look for? My hope is in you."

PSALM 39:6–7

Out of curiosity, I logged on to the Suicide Crisis Center Web site. Although I wouldn't normally visit this particular site, I wanted to see what counsel it offered to people contemplating suicide. After all, suicide is usually the result of utter hopelessness. So, I wondered, what hope would this Internet resource offer to those needing it most?

In my quest for information, I was drawn to two particular articles. One was titled, "Why Live? When You Feel Like Dying." Its answer to that question went like this:

- Because you have an illness that makes you want to kill yourself.

- Because you are not just depressed—you have depression. . . .

- Because you can treat depression, even cure it.

- Because your life has value and can be saved. . . .

- [Because] your life force wants you to go on, find treatment, and make a meaningful life for yourself and those you love or will love. [1]

In another article, the possible cures for depression are listed and evaluated. The article begins by stating, "Depression is a treatable illness. . . . Somehow, someway, you must change, improve, or correct your brain chemistry before you will feel good again."[2] It continues by listing several possible methods of treatment: antidepressants, psychotherapy, hormone treatment, nutritional supplementation, special clinics, L-Tryptophan, herbal remedies, ECT shock treatments, and alternative medicine. The list concludes with a very nebulous "religion" category and then adds, "Remember, it's great to pray, but get chemical help anyway!"

Interestingly, the Bible approaches hopelessness in any form—from suicide and depression to guilt and anxiety—in a very different way. Instead of categorizing despair as a psychological disease, the Bible simply calls it disobedience—a refusal to trust our faithful and loving God (Psalms 37:1–7, 56:3, 62:8; Proverbs 3:5). And, instead of promoting treatment plans, dietary pills, or chemical prescriptions, Scripture points people to the basis of true hope—namely, God Himself. Certainly, modern medical science plays a key role in caring for legitimate diseases and health conditions. Yet, when it comes to finding hope in this life, God's Word is clear: The source is always and only the Lord.

In fact, all throughout Scripture the concepts of hope, trust, promise, faith, belief, and confident expectation appear continually. They are like mile markers on the highway—signposts that constantly remind the reader to focus on God and look to Him for assistance. He is our refuge (Psalm 9:9), our joy (Psalm 43:4), our deliverer (Psalm 18:2), our help (Psalm 40:17), our strength (Psalm 22:19), and our comfort (Psalm 119:76). Why then would we hope in medication or therapy or anything else before we would hope in God?

Where then should we as Christians turn when life seems hopeless? Where should we look for hope when we're feeling discouraged or dismayed? The Bible gives us the obvious answer: We must look to the One whose promises are sure, whose power is unsurpassed, whose wisdom is eternal, and whose love is infinite. Whether we look to the provision of our heavenly Father, the Person of our Savior Jesus Christ, or the promises of Holy Scripture, the point remains: Hope is found in God alone. After all, Jesus Christ is God the Son, God in human flesh. And Holy Scripture is God's book, written by the Holy Spirit.

Let's turn our attention, then, to God's Word and be encouraged to look for hope where God tells us to find it. Let's see where our Creator, the One who made us and knows us best, wants us to go when we feel hopeless. And, while many other verses could be added to our list, be encouraged by this brief testimony of thirty biblical passages, given by God Himself, concerning where to find true hope.

You Can Find Hope by Looking to Your Heavenly Father

- PSALM 33:20–22: *We wait in hope for the LORD; he is our help and our shield. In him our hearts rejoice, for we trust in his holy name. May your unfailing love rest upon us, O LORD, even as we put our hope in you.*

- PSALM 62:5–8: *Find rest, O my soul, in God alone; my hope comes from him. He alone is my rock and my salvation;*

he is my fortress, I will not be shaken. My salvation and my honor depend on God; he is my mighty rock, my refuge. Trust in him at all times, O people; pour out your hearts to him, for God is our refuge.

- PSALM 71:5: *For you have been my hope, O Sovereign LORD, my confidence since my youth.*

- PSALM 146:5–6: *Blessed is he whose help is the God of Jacob, whose hope is in the LORD his God, the Maker of heaven and earth, the sea, and everything in them—the LORD, who remains faithful forever.*

- PSALM 147:10–11: *His [God's] pleasure is not in the strength of the horse, nor his delight in the legs of a man; the LORD delights in those who fear him, who put their hope in his unfailing love.*

- PROVERBS 23:17–18: *Do not let your heart envy sinners, but always be zealous for the fear of the LORD. There is surely a future hope for you, and your hope will not be cut off.*

- MICAH 7:7: *But as for me, I watch in hope for the LORD, I wait for God my Savior; my God will hear me.*

- 2 CORINTHIANS 1:10: *He [God] has delivered us from such a deadly peril, and he will deliver us. On him we have set our hope that he will continue to deliver us.*

- EPHESIANS 1:18: *I pray also that the eyes of your heart may be enlightened in order that you may know the hope to which he [God] has called you, the riches of his glorious inheritance in the saints.*

- 1 TIMOTHY 6:17: *Command those who are rich in this present world not to be arrogant nor to put their hope in wealth, which is so uncertain, but to put their hope in God, who richly provides us with everything for our enjoyment.*

- TITUS 1:1–2: *Paul, a servant of God and an apostle of Jesus Christ for the faith of God's elect and the knowledge of the truth that leads to godliness—a faith and knowledge resting on the hope of eternal life, which God, who does not lie, promised before the beginning of time.*

- HEBREWS 10:23: *Let us hold unswervingly to the hope we profess, for he who promised is faithful.*

* See also: Psalm 25:1–5; 31:23–24; 52:9; 65:5; 133:3; Isaiah 40:28–31; Romans 5:1–5; 2 Thessalonians 2:16–17; Hebrews 6:17–20; 1 Peter 1:3–4.

YOU CAN FIND HOPE BY LOOKING TO CHRIST AND HIS RETURN

- MATTHEW 12:21: *"In his [Jesus'] name the nations will put their hope."*

- ROMANS 15:12–13: *And again, Isaiah says, "The Root of Jesse will spring up, one who will arise to rule over the nations; the Gentiles will hope in him." May the God of hope fill you with all joy and peace as you trust in him, so that you may overflow with hope by the power of the Holy Spirit.*

- COLOSSIANS 1:3–5: *We always thank God, the Father of our Lord Jesus Christ, when we pray for you, because we have heard of your faith in Christ Jesus and of the love you have for all the saints—the faith and love that spring from the hope that is stored up for you in heaven and that you have already heard about in the word of truth, the gospel.*

- COLOSSIANS 1:27–28: *To them God has chosen to make known among the Gentiles the glorious riches of this mystery, which is Christ in you, the hope of glory. We proclaim him, admonishing and teaching everyone with all wisdom, so that we may present everyone perfect in Christ.*

- 1 THESSALONIANS 4:13–14: *Brothers, we do not want you to be ignorant about those who fall asleep, or to grieve like the rest of men, who have no hope. We believe that Jesus died and rose again and so we believe that God will bring with Jesus those who have fallen asleep in him.*

- 1 TIMOTHY 1:1: *Paul, an apostle of Christ Jesus by the command of God our Savior and of Christ Jesus our hope.*

- TITUS 2:11–14: *For the grace of God that brings salvation has appeared to all men. It teaches us to say "No" to ungodliness and worldly passions, and to live self-controlled, upright and godly lives in this present age, while we wait for the blessed hope—the glorious appearing of our great God and Savior, Jesus Christ, who gave himself for us to redeem us from all wickedness and to purify for himself a people that are his very own, eager to do what is good.*

- TITUS 3:4–7: *But when the kindness and love of God our Savior appeared, he saved us, not because of righteous things we had done, but because of his mercy. He saved us through the washing of rebirth and renewal by the Holy Spirit, whom he poured out on us generously through Jesus Christ our Savior, so that, having been justified by his grace, we might become heirs having the hope of eternal life.*

- 1 PETER 1:13: *Therefore, prepare your minds for action; be self-controlled; set your hope fully on the grace to be given you when Jesus Christ is revealed.*

- 1 JOHN 3:2–3: *Dear friends, now we are children of God, and what we will be has not yet been made known. But we know that when he [Christ] appears, we shall be like him, for we shall see him as he is. Everyone who has this hope in him purifies himself, just as he is pure.*

YOU CAN FIND HOPE BY LOOKING TO GOD'S WORD

- PSALM 119:43: *Do not snatch the word of truth from my mouth, for I have put my hope in your laws.*

- PSALM 119:49: *Remember your word to your servant, for you have given me hope.*

- PSALM 119:74: *May those who fear you rejoice when they see me, for I have put my hope in your word.*

- PSALM 119:81: *My soul faints with longing for your salvation, but I have put my hope in your word.*

- PSALM 119:114: *You are my refuge and my shield; I have put my hope in your word.*

- PSALM 119:147: *I rise before dawn and cry for help; I have put my hope in your word.*

- PSALM 130:5–7: *I wait for the LORD , my soul waits, and in his word I put my hope. My soul waits for the Lord more than watchmen wait for the morning, more than watchmen wait for the morning. O Israel, put your hope in the LORD, for with the LORD is unfailing love and with him is full redemption.*

- ROMANS 15:4: *For everything that was written in the past*

was written to teach us, so that through endurance and the
encouragement of the Scriptures we might have hope.

WHERE IS YOUR HOPE BUILT?

Clearly, the overwhelming testimony of Scripture is that lasting hope is found in God alone—whether through the provision of the Father, the Person of the Son, or the promises of Scripture. While people are often tempted to look elsewhere, their search for true hope is a vain endeavor. Medication may make them feel better, alcohol may dull their senses, entertainment may help them escape, other possibilities may distract them—yet, all of these are only temporary fixes. They are like bandages on cancer. They can never actually solve the problem, they can only cover it up for a time.

Only a heart that has been changed by Jesus Christ and that looks to God for its strength can enjoy true hope. The promises of God can be trusted because God cannot lie; they can be enjoyed because they were given for our spiritual good; and they can be embraced forever because they are eternal.

Are you discouraged? Are you disheartened and downcast? Is your life not what you desire? Is the guilt of your sin too much for you to bear? Do your problems feel insurmountable or your struggles too painful to endure? Do you not know that there is hope, real hope, in God? Jesus said, in Matthew 11:28, "Come to me, all you who are weary and burdened, and I will give you rest." The question is, will you come? Or, will you look for your hope in the things of this earth, things that can never satisfy and will ultimately only disappoint?

With this in mind, John Gill says:

God is faithful to all His promises, nor can He fail,
or deceive; He is all wise and foreknowing of everything

that comes to pass; He never changes His mind, nor for-
gets His word; and He is able to perform, and is the God
of truth, and cannot lie; nor has He ever failed in any
one of His promises, nor will He suffer [allow] His
faithfulness to fail; and this is a strong argument to hold
fast a profession of faith.[3]

Our search for help, then, must begin with the One who will never fail, for only He offers true hope.

CHAPTER 31

HOPE IS WHERE
YOUR HEART IS:

Final Application and Conclusion

"For where your treasure is, there your heart will be also."

MATTHEW 6:21

Take just a moment to think about this question before you answer it: If you could have anything you wanted, anything at all, what one thing would you choose?

Would it be exceeding wealth—more money than anyone in this world has ever had before? Or would it be incredible beauty and a dashing appearance? What about ultimate power—a position of international leadership and prestige? Maybe you would ask for a never-ending romance with the lover of your dreams; you might ask for impeccable health or an extraordinarily long life; or maybe you would simply desire a never-ending vacation in which you could travel to exotic locations around the world.

While the question itself may seem a bit fantastic, your answer is nonetheless significant—because it reveals the one thing you think would bring you greatest satisfaction. When it comes to what we want, we always choose what we think will make us most happy.

And, by declaring what we would wish for as our ultimate treasure—the one thing we would want more than anything else—we betray the true inclinations of our heart (Matthew 6:21).

Have you ever wondered how the apostle Paul might answer that question? What would he want if he could have anything his heart desired? Guessing aside, Paul tells us in his letters—more than anything else he would want the return of Jesus Christ.

Certainly Paul wanted the lost to be saved (Romans 10:1), and the church to be established (2 Corinthians 11:28). Clearly, he wanted to be faithful in his ministry (2 Corinthians 5:9–10). Yet, even more than living and ministering, he desired to go and be with Christ (Philippians 1:23). And, even more than going to be with Christ, he looked forward to when Christ would return to earth and all believers, everywhere, would receive their resurrection bodies (Philippians 3:7–11). Only then, at Christ's return, would the glorification process be finally completed. Only then would Paul's sinful body be replaced with a sinless one. In Paul's mind, being with Christ in spirit was better than anything on this earth; and the only thing better than that was to be with Christ in both spirit and resurrected body.

After all, Christ's return is the culmination of our hope; it will include everything we hope for—reward, resurrection, reign, rest, and perfect relationship with the Savior. Our hope will not be entirely complete until that moment. Yet, at His coming it will be fully realized—and it will remain that way for all eternity. Paul's greatest desire, then, was the return of his Master.

Paul explains all of this in Romans 8:18–23. In verse 18, he says, "I consider that our present sufferings are not worth comparing with the glory that will be revealed in us." Certainly, Paul knew what it was like to suffer. He had experienced severe persecution and difficulty (2 Corinthians 11:23–28), hunger and poverty (Philippians 4:10–19), emotional pain (2 Timothy 4:9–16), and the daily struggle with sin (Romans 7:8–24). Yet, when hard times came, he relied on God's strength and looked forward to a future time that only hope could see: the return of Christ—the time at which the glory of His resurrection power will be revealed in us (Philippians 3:10).

In the verses that follow (Romans 8:19–21), Paul identifies three facets of true hope—elements that should characterize the hope of every believer. He does this by comparing Christians with creation, noting that both groups have a vested interest in Jesus' return.

FACET #1:
YOUR HOPE SHOULD INCLUDE EXPECTATION

In Romans 8:19, Paul states that the creation, speaking metaphorically, "waits in eager expectation for the sons of God to be revealed." And, we as Christians are also to "wait eagerly" for "the redemption of our bodies" (v. 23).

But why does creation long for Jesus' return? Because, when He sets up His earthly kingdom, sin's curse on nature will be removed (compare Genesis 3:14–19 with Isaiah 65). In fact, 2 Peter 3:10–13 says that one day this entire earth will be replaced with a new one. So, for all of eternity, the creation will enjoy its full potential, being freed from the corruption of sin. Likewise, believers can look forward to Jesus' coming because their new bodies will also be free from sin's influence. Currently, we still feel the effects of the Fall (Genesis 3:14–19). But, when we receive our new bodies, our sinful flesh will no longer be with us. We will be free of it forever.

What's interesting is that in discussing these truths, Paul calls them an "expectation." They are not merely wishful fantasies or far-fetched dreams. Paul knows that his hope is a future reality. God has promised it as part of the inheritance of Romans 8:17. Jesus Christ has proven its trustworthiness—through His own resurrection (see 1 Corinthians 15:12–28). And the Holy Spirit has been given as a guarantee (see Romans 8:11, 23). Hope, then, is no experiment, but rather a confident expectation—based on the absolute certainties of God and His Word.

FACET #2:
YOUR HOPE SHOULD INCLUDE EXCITEMENT

Romans 8:19 and 23 reveal a second facet of Paul's hope. Not only was his hope a confident expectation, but it was also the essence of his joy and anticipation. For Paul, Jesus' return was not some sort of terrifying nightmare he hoped would never happen. It was not even an event that Paul wished could be delayed. The apostle eagerly expected that it could happen at any moment, the sooner the better. In verses 19 and 23 he characterizes the anticipation of both creation and the Christian as "eager."

How far this is from many in the church today, especially among young people. Yes, we say we want Jesus to return. . .but if He could only wait until I'm married, done with college, have a family, have a career, enjoy retirement, and so on. It is not until we are diagnosed with terminal cancer or some other disease that we long for Him to come.

But Paul knew that, no matter what stage of life he was in and no matter what earthly joys were in his future, the return of His Master would be far better. After all, even the most wonderful experiences we can have in this life are still tainted by sin. Yet, when Christ comes back, sin will be no more. Our resurrection bodies will be free from the struggles we face every day (see Romans 7:14–25). Moreover, we will be with Christ—the Source of satisfaction and the Lover of our souls. True happiness and ultimate fulfillment will be ours because sin will be gone and the Savior will be present. The best thing you can think of in this life cannot even compare to the joys of the next (Romans 8:18).

FACET #3:
YOUR HOPE SHOULD INCLUDE EXERTION

Paul continues, in Romans 8:20–23, to add a third facet of true hope to his list—namely, exertion. He says this, "We ourselves, who have the firstfruits of the Spirit, groan inwardly as we wait eagerly for our adoption as sons, the redemption of our bodies" (v. 23). So, the waiting period involves not only expectation and excitement, but also groaning and pain—pain caused by both persecution (see v. 17) and the sinful flesh (see vv. 5–13).

What Paul is saying, then, is that our hope is a motivation to persistence and endurance in this life. Temptation is all around us, our sinful lusts are within us, and our enemies are attacking us. Yet, we must not give up, because one day our Lord will appear. And we must not be lazy, because His reward is with Him (Revelation 22:12). And although the wait seems hard, we endure it diligently (see Romans 8:25).

Paul's illustration in verse 22 sums it up perfectly. He says that our struggle now is like the pains of childbirth. As a husband and father, I have witnessed my wife endure such pain—the anguish being so acute that no amount of coaching or breathing seemed to help. Yet, after our child was born, the joy of that new life far outweighed all of the hardship of labor. In the same way, while our exertion, effort, and endurance may seem great in the present, they are nothing compared to the glories of eternity.

How sad it is when Christians think of their hope as nothing more than eternal fire insurance—a policy that somehow allows them to live however they want in the present with no fear of the future. Yet, for Paul, the right perspective was just the opposite. Looking to the future caused him to despise the cheap thrills of sin and allowed him to endure the difficulties of persecution and tribulation. As Christians, we should share in that perspective.

Paul finishes this section of Romans 8 by saying, "For in this hope we were saved. But hope that is seen is no hope at all. Who hopes for what he already has? But if we hope for what we do not yet have, we wait for it patiently" (vv. 24–25). Paul admits that Christ's return is future. It is something we cannot see because it hasn't happened yet. Nevertheless, because it is guaranteed by God, we can wait for it with patient confidence. Knowing that His coming is certain means that we can live in light of it, even though it is still to come.

WHERE IS YOUR TREASURE?

David Livingstone (1813–1873) was a Scottish missionary and explorer of Africa, where he spent some thirty years of his life. Although famous for his many exploits and discoveries, Livingstone was also well known for his love of the African people. In fact, through his efforts, the slave trade was temporarily halted.

At his death, his body was sent back to Great Britain, where it was buried in Westminster Abbey. His heart, however, was not included with his remains. As he had requested before his death, it was re-moved while still in Africa and buried there. The reason being that, for Livingstone, the African people were his love and his prize. While his body belonged to Scotland by birth, his heart belonged to the continent he treasured.

In a similar sense, should the Lord tarry, our bodies will be buried in this earth. I wonder, however, if it were possible, how many of us could honestly have our hearts buried in heaven. How many of us are so focused on the hope that waits for us there—a hope that will climax with Christ's return—that our treasure really is in God and His kingdom.

When we put our stock in God and His promises, we will live with confident expectation, eager excitement, and patient exertion—as we allow the realities of our future to impact our present. However, when we invest primarily in the things of this earth, we will cling to this life as though it is the end as we look for happiness in things that can never satisfy. As Christians we have that choice. Like bums who are offered a royal feast, we can either savor the truth of God's Word or we can dig in the trash cans of this life. Hope offers us everything because it encompasses all that God has promised. How foolish we are when we chose to ignore it.

FAITH, HOPE, AND LOVE

In bringing this book to a close, there is one final thought that I wish to briefly address. It is Paul's statement in 1 Corinthians 13:13: "And now these three remain: faith, hope and love. But the greatest of these is love." In light of this, two questions must be answered.

First, what is the relationship of hope to faith and love? In this book, we have contended that hope refers to the promises that God gives His children. When used as a noun, it is, in fact, synonymous with promise or inheritance. Faith, by way of distinction, looks to the hope that God has promised and believes. In fact, when hope is used as a verb, it is nearly identical with faith—conveying the idea of confident trust. Love is the active result of faith—meaning that when we walk by faith we will automatically be walking in love. After all, love is the fulfillment of all that God expects of us (Mark 12:30–31; Romans 13:8–10). So, God promises (hope), and we believe (faith) and live accordingly (love).

A second question is this: What makes love greater than hope? I believe the answer to this question is simply this: While faith and hope will one day cease, love endures forever. Think of it—when Jesus returns or when we die and go to Him, our faith will be sight and our hope will be realized. God's promises will no longer be verbal guarantees, they will be physical realities. Our trust will no longer be without sight but will be rewarded before our very eyes.

Yet love will never end, it will only be heightened. The joy of heaven, in fact, will stem from the love of God for us and from our perfect love for Him, along with the perfect love we share with all the saints.

As believers, we can rejoice in knowing that our hope will not always be only a promise. Indeed, one day we will enjoy it as the reality that God says it will be. In the meantime, may our lives reflect what we know to be true and may our hearts find their treasure in heaven.

ENDNOTES

CHAPTER 1

[1] J. B. Nicholson, Jr., "My Father's House," *Uplook*, July 1998, 2. The letter was written to Charles Fuller by Dr. Harry Rimmer.

[2] Gary Thomas, "Wise Christians Clip Obituaries," *Christianity Today*, 3 October 1994, 24–26.

[3] Statistics from the Barna Research Group for 2001.

CHAPTER 4

[1] Maria C. Morog, *Reader's Digest*, December 1980, n.p.

[2] John Piper, *Desiring God* (Sisters, Ore.: Multnomah, 1996), 238.

CHAPTER 6

[1] C. S. Lewis, *The Problem of Pain* (New York: Macmillan, 1976), 144.

[2] D. L. Moody, *Moody's Anecdotes* (Chicago: Moody Press, n.d.), 125–26.

[3] J. I. Packer, *Your Father Loves You* (Colorado Springs: Harold Shaw Publishers, 1986), page for September 23.

[4] C. S. Lewis, *Mere Christianity* (New York: Macmillan, 1960), 119.

CHAPTER 7

[1] Paul Borthwick, "Adoniram Judson: Endurance Personified." Cited by Jonathan McRostie, "Comfort," *Linking Together*, n.d. *Linking Together* is the newsletter of Operation Mobilization's World Partners.

CHAPTER 8

[1] Andrew Murray. Cited by Amy Carmichael, *Though the Mountains Shake* (New York: Loizeaux Bros., 1946), 12.

[2] C. S. Lewis, *The Problem of Pain* (New York: Macmillan, 1976), 106.

[3] Augustine, *The Confessions of Saint Augustine*. Cited by David Koch, "Crowned with Lovingkindness," *CLF Newsletter* (17 February 1992), 3.

CHAPTER 9

[1] John M. Drescher, "Death," *Leadership Journal* (Summer 1985).

CHAPTER 11

[1] *American Heritage Dictionary of the English Language*, 4th ed. (Boston: Houghton Mifflin, 2000), s.v. "Worry."

[2] Charles Swindoll, *Questions Christians Ask* (Dallas, Tex.: Word Publishing, 1989), 18.

[3] Walter Kelly. Cited from "Anxiety," Sermon Illustrations Online, n.d., http://www.christianglobe.com/Illustrations (accessed February 8, 2003).

[4] Arthur T. Pierson, *George Mueller of Bristol* (Old Tappan, N.J.: Fleming H. Revell, 1899), 186.

CHAPTER 12

[1] Amy Bernstein, "Eye on the '90s," *U.S. News & World Report*, 27 July 1992, 11.

[2] *Our Daily Bread*, 18 May 1994. Story told by Philip Parham.

CHAPTER 13

[1] John Calvin, "On Meditating on the Future Life," in *The Institutes of the Christian Religion*, Book 3. This selection is a contemporary adaptation of material taken from chapter four of Calvin's work. It was originally translated from the French by Henry Beveridge in 1845 for the Calvin Translation Society.

CHAPTER 14

[1] Quotations cited from Randy Alcorn, *The Treasure Principle* (Sisters, Ore.: Multnomah, 2001).

[2] Ibid.

[3] Benjamin Franklin, *Benjamin Franklin Wit and Wisdom* (White Plains, N.Y.: Peter Pauper Press, 1998).

[4] Abraham Lincoln, *Wit and Wisdom of Abraham Lincoln* (White Plains, N.Y.: Peter Pauper Press, 1998).

[5] John MacArthur, "The Believer's Life in Christ" (Valencia, Calif.: Grace to You): Tape # GC 1905.

[6] Patrick Henry. Cited from Randy Wolff, "God's Will for Your Life—A Choice," *Our Daily Light* (Estes Park, Colo.: Fireside Ministries, n.d.), page for December 31.

CHAPTER 16

[1] Leslie Flynn, *The Sustaining Power of Hope* (Wheaton, Ill.: Scripture Press, 1985), 27–28.

[2] Ibid.

CHAPTER 17

[1] J. I. Packer, *Your Father Loves You* (Colorado Springs: Harold Shaw Publishers, 1986), page for May 14.

[2] Biblical Studies Foundation, "Heaven," http://www.bible.org (accessed March 15, 2003).

[3] F. B. Meyer. Cited by Mrs. C. Cowman, *Consolation* (Los Angeles: Oriental Mission Society, 1945), 70.

[4] *Today in the Word*, April 10, 1993. *Today in the Word* is a daily devotional provided by Moody Bible Institute.

[5] Cited by Woodrow Kroll, *Early in the Morning* (Neptune, N.J.: Loizeaux Brothers, 1994), page for June 19.

CHAPTER 19

[1] Arthur T. Pierson, *George Muller of Bristol and His Witness to a Prayer Hearing God*, 460. Cited in *Grace in Focus*, 2/3 (May/June 1996): 4.

CHAPTER 20

[1] C. S. Lewis, *Reflections on the Psalms* (New York: Harcourt, Brace, 1958), 80.

[2] Richard Baxter, *The Saints' Everlasting Rest* (Westwood, N.J.: Revell, 1962), chapter 16.

CHAPTER 23

[1] Jerry Bridges, *Trusting God* (Colorado Springs, Colo.: NavPress, 1988), 195.

CHAPTER 24

[1] John R. W. Stott, *The Preacher's Portrait* (Grand Rapids: Wm. B. Eerdmans, 1961), 120.

[2] J. C. Ryle, *Holiness* (Moscow, Idaho: Charles Nolan, 2001 Reprint), 56–57.

[3] Jerry Bridges, *The Pursuit of Holiness* (Colorado Springs, Colo.: NavPress, 1978), 145.

[4] John Piper, *A Godward Life* (Sisters, Ore.: Multnomah, 1997), 125.

CHAPTER 25

[1] *Webster's Revised Unabridged Dictionary* (Micra Inc., 1998), s.v. "Faith."

[2] Charles Spurgeon, "Is God in the Camp?" A sermon on 1 Samuel 4:7. Preached April 9, 1891, at the Metropolitan Tabernacle. Sermon No. 2239.

[3] John Bunyan, *Pilgrim's Progress* (New York: The Macmillan Company, 1907). This account has been adapted from the original in order to make it easier to read.

[4] Warren Wiersbe, *Wycliffe Handbook of Preaching & Preachers* (Chicago: Moody Press, 1984), 242.

CHAPTER 28

[1] Eugene H. Merrill, *Kingdom of Priests* (Grand Rapids: Baker, 1996), 26.

[2] Flavius Josephus, *Antiquities of the Jews*, 1:7.

CHAPTER 30

[1] Melody Clark, "Why Live? When You Feel Like Dying," http://www.suicidecrisiscenter.com (accessed May 10, 2003).

[2] Melody Clark, "Question 12: What Treatments Are Available for Depression?" http://www.depressionfaq.com/q12.html (accessed May 10, 2003).

[3] John Gill, *Exposition of the Entire Bible* (Philadelphia: W. W. Woodward, 1811), comment on Hebrews 10:23.

If you enjoyed

Living a Life of Hope
be sure to check out the following books,
also available from Barbour Publishing, Inc.

My Utmost for His Highest
ISBN 1-57748-914-4
Hardback, 288 pages, $9.97

Prayers & Promises for Men
ISBN 1-58660-833-9
Printed Leatherette, 224 pages, $4.97

Prayers & Promises for Women
ISBN 1-58660-832-0
Printed Leatherette, 224 pages, $4.97

Come Away My Beloved
ISBN 1-58660-576-3
Hardback, 256 pages, $14.99

Available wherever books are sold.